PENGUIN BOOKS

SEX AND LIES

Leila Slimani is the bestselling author of *The Perfect Nanny*, one of *The New York Times Book Review*'s 10 Best Books of the Year, and *Adèle*, for which she won the La Mamounia Prize. A journalist and frequent commentator on women's and human rights issues, she spearheaded a campaign—for which she won the Simone de Beauvoir Prize for women's freedom—to help Moroccan women speak out, as self-declared outlaws, against their country's "unfair and obsolete laws." She is French president Emmanuel Macron's personal representative for the promotion of the French language and culture and was ranked number two on *Vanity Fair* France's annual list of the Fifty Most Influential French People in the World. Born in Rabat, Morocco, in 1981, she now lives in Paris with her French husband and their two young children.

Also by Leila Slimani

THE PERFECT NANNY
ADÈLE

SEX
AND
LIES

TRUE STORIES OF
WOMEN'S INTIMATE LIVES
IN THE ARAB WORLD

LEILA
SLIMANI

Translated from the French by
Sophie Lewis

 **PENGUIN BOOKS**

PENGUIN BOOKS

An imprint of Penguin Random House LLC

penguinrandomhouse.com

First published in Great Britain by Faber and Faber Ltd. 2020

Published in Penguin Books 2020

Originally published in French as *Sexe et mensonges* by Éditions des Arènes, Paris

ISBN 9780143133766 (paperback)
ISBN 9780525505594 (ebook)

Printed in the United States of America
10 9 8 7 6 5 4 3 2 1

Set in Minion Pro

In memory of Fatima Mernissi;
For my Aunt Atika;
For all the women who confided in me:
this is to thank you.

Preaching chastity is an open incitement to anti-nature. Disdain for sexual life and sullying it with the notion of 'impurity', such is the true sin against the Holy Spirit of life.

Friedrich Nietzsche, *The Antichrist*

When Allah created the earth, said Father, he separated men from women, and put a sea between Muslims and Christians for a reason. Harmony exists when each group respects the prescribed limits of the other; trespassing leads only to sorrow and unhappiness. But women dreamed of trespassing all the time. The world beyond the gate was their obsession. They fantasised all day long about parading in unfamiliar streets.

Fatima Mernissi, *Dreams of Trespass*

CONTENTS

PREFACE 2020

Sex and Lies was first published in 2017, in French. The book triggered bitter discussion in Morocco, and there were many activists, sociologists and intellectuals who joined me in decrying the state of sexual freedom in our country. More books were published and debates were televised but the laws themselves saw no change. Instead, a series of scandals and arbitrary arrests was reported across the kingdom. In 2019 a famous actress was arrested for adultery after her husband reported her. A senior civil servant was caught in a Marrakesh hotel bedroom with his mistress, who, when the police arrived, threw herself out of the window. Worst of all, upon leaving a clinic in September 2019, the journalist Hajar Raissouni was arrested and, along with her doctor, charged with participating in a clandestine pregnancy termination and with pursuing sexual relations outside marriage. Raissouni, who at the time was working for a newspaper well known for its criticism of the status quo and whose family includes a number of high-profile figures in political Islamism, rapidly became an icon for the campaign for sexual freedom. Observing this proliferation of cases, the film director Sonia Terrab and I decided to launch our manifesto for those obliged to live outside the law. It seemed to us that the systemic hypocrisy prevailing throughout our country had to be exposed. Because, although sexual relations outside marriage are forbidden by law, they are nonetheless practised every day and by everyone, whatever their social background. Moroccans' motto is simple: Do what you wish, but never talk about it. So Sonia and I rounded up our friends and our wider social circles; we called on artists, intellectuals and politicians, male and female. On 23 September, dozens of publications printed our manifesto, which had collected almost five hundred signatures.

Over the days that followed, more than twenty thousand people contacted us wanting to join our project. Thousands of women sent us their stories and, through them, we discovered the true scale of the situation. Humiliation at the hands of the police; backstreet abortions; mistrustful doctors refusing to treat women in emergency conditions due to fear of the authorities; and the violent arrests of people in cars and hotels. We discovered the degree to which the Moroccan people are sick of the injunction to lie about their private lives. The degree too to which our repressive laws are increasingly utilised arbitrarily to buy others' silence, to blackmail unwelcome neighbours and to exact revenge on the perpetrators of any disservice. Many of Morocco's citizens have come to realise that the laws themselves are responsible for the shadow, the constant threat that holds them back. And they know too that it's the poorest, the most vulnerable and the women in particular who pay the greatest price for this sexual repression, while the well-off are able to live their sex lives more or less as they wish.

This growing awareness gives me hope. Like young people across the whole region, in Algeria, Tunisia and Egypt, the young people of Morocco are hungry for freedom; they want to see their right to a private life respected. The battle goes on, more urgently than ever.

INTRODUCTION

When, in the summer of 2014, I published my first novel, *Adèle*, some French journalists expressed surprise that a Moroccan woman could write such a book. What they meant by that was an 'unconstrained book', a 'sexy book', a straight-talking, popular book, the story of a woman suffering from sex addiction. As if, by culture, I should have been more prudish, more reserved. As if I should have made do with writing an erotic novelette with orientalist shades, worthy scion of Scheherazade that I am.

Yet I feel that North Africans are well placed to take on themes relating to sexual suffering, frustration and alienation. The fact of living or having grown up in societies without sexual freedom makes sex a subject of constant obsession. Besides, sex is one issue that's well represented in contemporary North African writing. It's there in the autobiographical novels of Mohamed Choukri, in the poetry and novels of Tahar Ben Jelloun, in the novels and criticism of Mohamed Leftah and in the novels and films about gay life of Abdellah Taïa. Erotic, even steamy, literature continues to be reinvented particularly among women, such as Lebanese writer Joumana Haddad and Syrian writer Salwa Al Neimi, whose novel *The Proof of the Honey* became a bestseller, following in the footsteps of the mysterious Nedjma, eponymous protagonist of the novel by Kateb Yacine.

So my first novel is in no way exceptional. I can even say it's no accident that I created a character like Adèle – a frustrated woman who lies and leads a double life. She's a woman eaten by regrets and by her own hypocrisy, a woman who steps out of line yet never experiences pleasure. Adèle is, in a way, a rather extreme metaphor for the sexual experience of young Moroccan women.

When my novel was published, I insisted on doing a book tour around Morocco, to present my book in several of the country's cities. I visited bookshops, universities and libraries. I accepted invitations from charities and support groups. The two weeks of my tour were a true revelation. I had never doubted the hunger for debate among those I was going to meet, but at every one of my encounters I was struck by how a discussion on the subject of sex enthused people, especially younger people. After the sessions, many, many women came up to me wanting to talk, to tell me their stories. Novels have a magical way of forging a very intimate connection between writers and their readers, of toppling the barriers of shame and mistrust. My hours with those women were very special. And it's their stories I have tried to give back: the impassioned testimonies of a time and of its suffering.

My intention here is not to document a sociological study nor to write an essay about sex in Morocco. Eminent sociologists and brilliant journalists are already doing this enormously delicate work. What I want is to render these women's words directly, as they were spoken to me: their intense and resonant speech, the stories that shook me, upset me, that angered and sometimes disgusted me. I want to give these often painful angles on life a platform in a society where many men and women prefer to turn away. By telling me their life stories, by choosing to break taboos, all of these women showed one thing, at least: that their lives matter. They should and do count. By confiding in me, they chose, if only for a few hours, to step out of isolation and to invite other women to realise that they're not alone. This is what makes their accounts political, committed, liberating. At the time of these encounters, I often returned to Moroccan sociologist Fatima Mernissi's remarks about Scheherazade – a superb figure but also, at times, a burdensome precedent for Muslim women: 'She would cure the troubled King's soul simply by talking to him about things that had happened to others . . . She would help him see his prison, his obsessive hatred of women.'* If, for Mernissi, Scheherazade appears a magnificent character, this isn't because she embodies the sensual and seductive oriental woman. On the contrary: it is because she reclaims her right to tell her own tale that she becomes not merely the object but the subject of the story. Women must rediscover ways of imposing their presence in a culture that remains hostage to religious and patriarchal authority. By speaking up, by telling their stories, women

* *Dreams of Trespass: Tales of a Harem Girlhood*

employ one of their most potent weapons against wide-spread hate and hypocrisy: words.

It's important to recognise quite how brave the women who speak out in this book have been, quite how difficult it is, in a country like Morocco, to step out of line, to embrace behaviour that is considered unconventional. Moroccan society relies entirely on the notion of community dependence. And the community is considered by its members as both inevitable, a fate they cannot dodge, and a piece of good fortune, since they can always count on it for a kind of group solidarity. So our relationship to our community remains profoundly ambivalent. Another cornerstone of Moroccan society is the concept of *hshouma*, which translates as 'shame' or 'embarrassment', and which is inculcated in every one of us from birth. To be well brought up, an obedient child, a good citizen, also means being alive to shame and regularly to demonstrate modesty and restraint. 'Harmony exists when each group respects the prescribed limits of the other; trespassing leads only to sorrow and unhappiness,' Mernissi wrote. The price of transgression is very high and anyone guilty of crossing the *hudud* – the 'sacred boundaries' – is punished accordingly and summarily rejected. The women who spoke to me have experienced only what befalls most Moroccans: an appalling, devastating inner conflict between the urge to shake off the tyranny of the community and the fear that freedom would bring all the traditional architecture of their world crashing down. All of them, as you will see, reveal ambivalence from time to time; they contradict themselves, claim their freedom then lower their eyes. They are trying to survive.

Listening to these women, I became determined to shine a light on the reality of this land, which is far more complex and more troubled than we are led to believe. For if we adhere to the rules as they stand and to morality as it is taught, we would have to assume that all Morocco's unmarried men are virgins. That all the young men and women, who represent more than half the population, have never had sexual intercourse. Cohabiting partners, homosexuals, prostitutes: all of these therefore could not exist at all. If we listen to our most conservative voices, anxious to defend a Moroccan identity made up more of myth than of reality, Morocco is a decent and virtuous country that must protect itself from the westernised decadence and liberalism of its elites. In Morocco, the ban on 'fornication', or *zina*, isn't just a moral injunction. Article 490 of the penal code prescribes 'imprisonment of between one month and one year [for] all persons of opposite sexes who, not being united by the bonds of marriage, pursue sexual relations'. According to article 489, all 'preferential or unnatural behaviour between two persons of the same sex will be punished by between six months and three years' imprisonment'. In a country where abortion is illegal except in cases of rape, severe embryo deformity or incest, and where 'all married persons proven guilty of adultery' risk between one and two years of prison (article 491), small-scale disasters occur every day. We don't see them, we don't hear them, and yet personal tragedies lie in wait for Morocco's citizens, many of whom feel as though this society that judges and rejects them is fundamentally hypocritical.

Of course, as everyone knows, the truth is that the laws governing us are flouted every hour of every day and at every level of society. Everyone knows it – but no one will acknowledge or confront it. The law against extramarital sexual relations is not respected, but the authorities absolutely refuse to admit this publicly. They know that hundreds of backstreet abortions take place every day, but the law against termination has only been minimally reformed. They must know that homosexual Moroccans live in fear and humiliation but they pretend not to. All those in positions of authority – politicians, parents, teachers – maintain the same line: 'Do what you like, but do it in private.'

In a society like ours, honour comes first. It isn't so much people's sex lives that we judge but how widely they dare to advertise them. Yet this command to silence is no longer enough to maintain social equilibrium and at the same time allow individuals' personal development. Our society has been eroded by the poison of its hypocrisy and by an institutionalised culture of lying. This combination engenders violence and confusion, inconsistency and intolerance. Staunch liberals are promoting the status quo alongside traditionalists. They seem to agree on the groundless conviction that Moroccan society isn't ready to progress on these questions.

But when women in miniskirts are being accused of gross indecency, when homosexuals are being lynched in broad daylight, then we urgently need to consider shaping a new society that can unite us and enable us to avoid these kinds of outrages. Like the other Muslim countries of North Africa, Morocco cannot afford to sidestep such self-examination. In an era when Islamic terrorism is ever more destructive, when Moroccan society is, like other Muslim societies, profoundly divided over questions of morality, I feel we can no longer disregard them. We can no longer allow ourselves to ignore the truth on the pretext that it does not conform to our religion, to our laws or simply to the image of ourselves that we'd like to project. We must stop giving in to the temptation to wash our hands of the matter, to the lazy definition of our culture and identity as fixed, supra-historical facts. We are not the same as our culture; rather, our culture is what we make of it. We need to stop pitting Islam and universal Enlightenment values against each other, stop opposing Islam and equality of the sexes, Islam and sensual pleasure. For the Muslim religion can be understood as primarily an ethics of liberation, of openness to the other, as a personal ethics and not only a Manichaean moral code.

More than ever, I am convinced that we need a complete overhaul of personal and sexual rights if we want to encourage young people's development and the proper involvement of women in society. We must, at least, initiate a collective rethink, without polemics and without hatred. What place do we want for the individual in our society? How can we protect women and minorities? How can we make difference acceptable in a society that prioritises adherence to religious norms and social monitoring? And what about the right to a private life, a personal space ruled neither by the state nor by religion?

I know that, for some, sexual rights and freedoms appear trivial. You might think that in a country like Morocco we've plenty of other battles to fight, that education, health and the struggle against poverty should come before personal freedoms. But sexual rights are a part of human rights; these are not minor rights, small boons that we can do without. To practise one's sexual citizenship, to do with our bodies as we see fit, to lead a sex life without risk, one that brings pleasure and is free from coercion: these are fundamental needs and rights that ought to be inalienable and guaranteed for all.

It's not just that sexual rights are part of human rights: we know that it's by exploiting the lack of them that men have come to dominate in so many civilisations. To defend sexual rights is directly to defend women's rights. Behind the right to control our own bodies, the right to live independently of our families in order to flourish in our sex lives, it is political rights that are at stake. By legislating in these areas, we will give women the means to defend themselves against male violence and familial pressure. The situation has become untenable. That is: this condition of generalised sexual privation, especially among women, whose sexual needs other than for reproduction are quite simply ignored, who are committed to compulsory virginity before marriage and to passivity thereafter. A woman whose body is subject to such severe social control cannot fully take her place as a citizen. And being 'sexualised' to such a degree, and constrained to silence or atonement, women are denied all individuality.

Michel Foucault wrote in *The History of Sexuality* that sexuality is 'a dense transfer point for relations of power: between men and women, young and old, parents and offspring, teachers and students, priests and laity, an administration and a population'. In Morocco, as in other Muslim countries, we can view this condition of sexual deprivation as an obstacle to the development of individuals and citizens. Kept in order by an iron-fisted government, men reproduce the authoritarian regime in their family circles and households. Thus we produce individuals adapted to an oppressive system. As the political commentator Omar Saghi remarked in an article in *Jeune Afrique*, sexual secrecy and political secrecy go hand in hand. 'Those who, at age sixteen, have had to beg a cop not to haul them in just because they were holding hands and because the family would be equally hard-line on this point, as brutal as our police state, are shaped by and for a life disfigured by dictatorships.'*

* *Jeune Afrique*, 30 January 2013

SORAYA[*]

'DON'T FORGET'

It was she who approached me. I was sitting at the bar in a chic hotel in Rabat. She came up to me, laid a hand on the seat next to mine and asked if she could sit there. I said: 'Yes, of course', simultaneously surprised and persuaded by her self-assurance. She sat down, smiling and ready to talk. She began to chat about this and that, apparently anxious not to leave a moment for the embarrassment that could arise between two unacquainted women having a drink together.

She talked about my book, at first. That's how we'd ended up meeting: thanks to this novel that she had read and wanted me to autograph, after the launch event that had just finished in the hotel's conference rooms. She had arrived late and been unable to join the discussion. When she'd reached the room, the talk was already over, the books signed, and I had disappeared. A member of staff had been kind enough to let her know I had gone to the bar, where I was enjoying a moment of solitude, a little respite. This was how she'd come to sit down beside me.

She must have been in her forties, an attractive woman, though rather unkempt. She hadn't looked after either her

[*] This name has been changed.

hair or her skin. Her nails were all shapes and lengths and she was smoking like a chimney. But her smile – her wide and infinitely sincere smile – transformed her. She smiled on an impulse of peculiar generosity, and now and then she would laugh, a childlike, naughty laugh. A laugh like crumpling a page that made her look down a little. She avoided all seriousness, seemed not to register pathos at all. At several points, I found her beautiful.

She began, of her own accord, to tell her story. I hardly dared to move. I left my glass where it was, didn't take a sip, afraid that a single movement might interrupt the flow of her disclosures. She asked me if I have a child. I replied that I do. *I haven't had any. I didn't manage it. It's the big regret of my life.* She then explained that she had been married very young, to a jealous and controlling man. They had tried for years to have children. She had had many miscarriages, had undergone treatments, then had given up. This failure had put an end to their marriage. *And besides, he wasn't very nice*, she said to me, laughing.

She hadn't been out with any other men before her husband. *When I was young, I was very square. I remember, when I was twenty, my college friends were totally wild. They would talk about their lovers, they even told us details of their sex lives. I felt very awkward about all of that. I was a virgin and basically very repressed.* After Soraya's divorce, she had gathered a new group of freethinking, uninhibited girlfriends with whom she could talk about everything. The freedom of their discussions, the licentiousness even, during her afternoons with the girls, had surprised and reassured her. These women explained how to become expert in the art of seducing men, they taught her ways to make them go crazy physically, even going as far as using strange potions.

Things were very different in my family, Soraya confessed to me. Then she described her mother. *She was a queen. A strong and beautiful woman, and highly disciplinarian.* And her mother had maintained an exclusively close relationship with Soraya's father. *My two sisters and I were hardly allowed to talk to him. As soon as we spotted the opportunity for a moment with him alone, she would call us into the kitchen or somewhere else to help her. She couldn't stand the idea of his loving anyone other than her.*

This adored and feared mother was determined that her daughters be good students, well integrated and sociable. She didn't stop them attending birthday tea parties or going out in the evenings or even spending the night at a girlfriend's house. *She trusted us, I think. But when she said goodbye, before dropping me off wherever it might be, she always leaned towards me and whispered into my ear: 'Don't forget.'* The young woman laughed, her tone at once affectionate and sad.

'What did she want you not to forget?' I dared to ask.

'Don't forget to stay a virgin.' That's what she was telling me. And that awful, sacred, constantly repeated command had become a potent refrain, a voice she could never shake off. *I wanted to loosen up this body. After my divorce – which my mother considered a terrible mark of failure – I felt strong,*

capable of taking my life in hand. I had the strange intuition that my body had much to offer, I wanted to discover pleasure, freedom. I never got there.

She did, however, meet an older man, someone she describes as sensual and patient. They made love often, taking their time. He tried to persuade her to 'let herself go'. *I was trying*, she assures me. *I was trying with all my heart, but I couldn't quite do it.*

For the last few minutes, I've had the feeling that she's prevaricating. That all these stories of hers are powerful and beautiful, but they're not the heart of the matter. This woman has a secret. I take out a cigarette and offer her one. My lighter is jammed; now the flint's making my thumb sore. She turns to the man sitting next to us and asks for a light. *Like that*, she says. *That's how it began. I turned to him and asked him for a light. He lit my cigarette and, as I was sitting alone and so was he, he suggested I join him. He just started talking. He told me his life story as if I were a friend, as if he trusted me implicitly. I was completely transfixed. I was fascinated by this man, to such a degree that it frightened me. I wanted to stay there forever, listening to him, and at the same time I was thinking I should be making for the door right away. He was articulate – and direct.*

Flushed, her eyes suddenly haunted, she confesses that at this point her husband – they were not yet divorced – began to call her phone and that, for the first time in her life, she rejected every call and ended up turning her phone off. She and the man talked for hours. She was slightly drunk when, around eleven o'clock, he suggested they go back to his place for a last drink and a kiss. And for all that would follow. She didn't dare. She took fright and fled, like a madwoman, without explanation. On the way home, she called a friend and asked him to be her alibi, to pretend they'd spent the evening at the cinema. She memorised the plot of the film they'd shown that evening and then recited it back to her husband word for word. At this she starts to laugh and adds with forced insouciance: *I signed my own death warrant. And yet I know it was worth it.*

*

I left Morocco more than fifteen years ago. With the years and the distance, I have surely forgotten quite how difficult it is to live without the freedoms that have become so natural to me. In France it can be a struggle to imagine the disorientation that comes with a young girl's discovery of her sexual self in a country where Islam is the state religion and the laws are extremely conservative on everything that relates to sex.

I am Moroccan and, in Morocco, Muslim laws apply to me, whatever my personal relationship with the religion. When I was a teenager, even though this went against their personal convictions, my parents must have explained to me that it was forbidden to have sexual relations outside marriage or even to be seen in a public place with a man who wasn't from my family. I learned that I could not be homosexual, have an abortion or cohabit. Being unable to have an abortion, if I were to have a child without being married, I could face criminal charges and my child would have no legal status; they would be a bastard. The new 'Family Code' of 2004 allows a child born outside marriage to be registered, but if the father will not acknowledge it the mother must choose the child's name from a list, all including the prefix *abd*, meaning 'servant', 'slave' or 'subordinate'. Born of an unknown father, the child will be a societal outcast and subject to social and economic exclusion. To avoid this exclusion and not risk arrest for an extramarital relationship, hundreds of women abandon children born outside wedlock. According to the Moroccan charity Insaf, in 2010 alone, twenty-four babies on average were abandoned every day, which adds up to almost nine thousand babies per year without identity or family, not to mention the corpses found in public bins.

In short, then: there's no salvation for the unmarried. For, while society is indulgent when it comes to the male body – which should be jubilant – all life outside marriage is forbidden to women. The law is hard but it is the law. Of course, the reality is different and many people bend the rules. Even the police, though employed to enforce the rule of law, are often happy to resolve a problem by accepting a few banknotes. You've only to step inside a nightclub in Marrakesh, Casablanca or Rabat to see this in action. But all of this creates a climate of confusion and stress – because it is profoundly arbitrary. And because you need only, just once, to be in the wrong place at the wrong time and be seen there by the wrong person. Depending on whether you are rich or poor, whether you live in a big city or a traditional village, the law will not apply to you in the same way as to others.

As a teenager, I realised that my sex life was everybody's business: society was entitled to control it. Virginity is an obsession in Morocco and throughout the Arab world. Whether you're liberal or not, religious or not, it's impossible to escape this obsession. According to the Family Code, before she is married a woman is meant to provide a 'certificate of unmarried status'. Of course, the man's virginity, which is impossible to prove and which isn't in demand anyway,

The 'Family Code' allows a child born outside marriage to be registered, but if the father will not acknowledge it the mother must choose the child's name from a list, all including the prefix *abd*, **meaning 'servant', 'slave' or 'subordinate'.**

bothers nobody. In street parlance, the expressions used for losing your virginity are revealing. During my discussions with women, many of them described girls who were no longer virgins as 'broken', 'spoiled' or 'ruined' by men, and said that this had to be managed as a terrible 'scar'.

Becoming an adult woman is a path mined with humiliations. When dealing with the police, with the justice system, even simply negotiating everyday public space, being a woman is a disadvantage. As the Turkish writer Zülfü Livaneli writes in his novel *Bliss*, 'All over the Mediterranean, the concept of honour is still considered to lie between a woman's thighs.' A heavy burden for half the population to shoulder. Idealised and mythologised, virginity has clearly become a coercive instrument intended to keep women at home and to justify their surveillance at all times. Far more than a personal question, it is the object of collective anxiety. It has also become a financial windfall for all those who carry out the dozens of hymen restorations that happen every day and for the labs selling false hymens, designed to bleed on the first day of sexual intercourse. Sexual deprivation, as we shall see, amounts to a capitalist system like any other.

When I was a teenager, everyone I knew could be split into two groups: those who were doing it and those who weren't. The choice, for us, cannot be compared to that made by young women in the West because in Morocco it is tantamount to a political statement, however unwitting. By losing her virginity, a woman automatically tips over into criminality, which of course is no laughing matter. But making this choice is not enough: you have to be able actually to realise your wish – and the obstacles are legion. Where can lovers meet? At the parents' house? Quite simply unthinkable. At a hotel? Even for those who might have the means, this is impossible, for hotels are known to demand a marriage certificate for couples wishing to share a room. So we find ourselves in cars, in forests, on the edges of beaches, on building sites or in empty lots. And accompanied by the appalling fear of being found and then arrested on the spot by the police. I don't know if a sixteen-year-old European girl can really imagine the stress such a situation can present.

I have experienced it. During my final year at school, I was in a car flirting with a boy. An innocent and entirely natural flirtation between two teenagers. A police car stopped a few metres away. The policemen walked up to our car. They knew perfectly well what we were up to. That was precisely why they were doing rounds of the forest. Everyone knew that dozens of couples could be found there every day: young and old, adulterous couples and schoolchildren in love, rich and poor, all propelled by the wish for a little intimacy in the shade of the eucalyptus trees. The police who patrol there are not a morality brigade but they behave like one. In fact, they don't give a toss what you're up to, if you're consenting or not; they don't take the time to make sure you are safe. They just show up like sheep to apply a law, or rather to take advantage of the profits. Because, in most cases, they don't mind looking the other way in exchange for a few notes. This is the price of your humiliation.

Around me, the boys mapped out a cruel geography. On one side were the 'nice girls' and on the opposite side . . . 'the others'. All day long they went on about how 'nice girls don't

smoke', 'nice girls don't go out in the evening . . . aren't friends
with boys . . . don't wear shorts . . . don't drink in public . . .
don't speak up before their brothers . . . don't dance in front
of men . . .' But I knew that nice girls aren't always the ones
we think they are. Like everyone else, I had heard that some
girls agreed to have anal sex rather than lose their virginity. I
didn't understand this notion of purity. To tell the truth, I'd
never felt that I was pure – ever. The paradox of the situation:
having so long considered women to be dangerous provoca-
teurs, people whose sexual appetite must constantly be kept
in check, we undermine the very concept of this purity we're
seeking to preserve. I felt guilty before I had even sinned.

The Lebanese poet and journalist Joumana Haddad talks
brilliantly about the important role played by education in
the perpetuation of misogyny and discrimination. She particularly addresses mothers who, all too often, bring their
sons up like demigods and, however open-minded they
may be themselves, tend to feel that their daughters should
appear docile and accept their lot. Following the sexual
assaults in Cologne on 31 December 2015, Haddad wrote
this in an opinion piece: 'Sorry to break it to you like this
– to you mothers – but if your sons are growing up to be
stalkers and rapists, to be violent, hopeless, bad husbands
and macho pigs, it isn't solely the fault of our society and
culture: you too are responsible. Listen, then, to this modest advice from a mother of two males: instead of telling

your daughter over and over that she's a target, stop telling your son that he's a hunter. Instead of teaching your daughter to keep quiet, try teaching your son to listen. If you're doing your best to give your daughter self-respect, try also to make sure that your son respects women. Instead of forbidding your daughter from wearing a skirt, try to make your son understand that a skirt is not an invitation to sex. Instead of forcing your daughter to cover up, try explaining to your son that a woman is more than just her body.'*

My father had three daughters: free, outspoken, independent women. For him, born in Fez in the 1940s, it can't have been easy to watch his daughters grow up in a society where women's role had changed completely but where powerful safeguards remained in place. He was constantly trying to strike a balance between passing on what he dearly believed in – that is, equality of the sexes – and the need to prepare us for the conservatism of the dominant morality. Sometimes, it was we who pressed for more freedom, we who persuaded him that our desire for freedom was greater than our need for protection. And I'm sure that in the course of his life, his view of women, but also of the issues associated with being a woman in this world, must have evolved substantially. We educated him just as he educated us. Together, we all brought each other up.

* 'Apres Cologne: le viol et nos hommes', *Les Nouvelles NEWS*, 20 January 2016

NOUR

'I'M NOT ASKING FOR THE MOON, JUST TO LIVE AS I WISH, WITH WHOEVER I WISH'

In Agadir, I was contacted by a brand-new charity whose project is to widen young people's horizons by offering them cultural activities. The head of the charity holds gatherings several times a week. He discusses films or literature with the young people or plays them pieces of music. When he wrote asking me to come and talk about my book, I didn't hesitate.

This is where I meet Nour. This elegant, middle-class thirty-something's story moves me a great deal. Very gentle and modest, she nonetheless shows a powerful urge to confide.

She begins by talking about her family. A single woman, she is still living with her parents. She says that her father is: *flexible, though he's still a Moroccan*. When I ask her what she means by that, she adds, a little shyly: *He cares a lot about what other people think. But he does give me some freedom. I'm allowed to do more than other girls in my family. He has never put his foot down completely; he usually agrees to discuss things and tells me his reasons. But he doesn't always. For example, I've never understood why he doesn't want me to take sports lessons. All I know is that, because of him, I've never taken any.*

My mother is a housewife. She is my father's first cousin. She left school just before her baccalaureate so she could get married. I think that made her very unhappy. She used to love school. As a result, she cares a lot about our schooling. She has always pushed me. I'm very close to my mother. I tell her almost everything, she's very open-minded. I even talk about my boyfriends, though not in detail, of course. I never talk about sex with my parents. For them, I'll be a virgin on my wedding day. My mother knows there have been people. But we're used to not talking about that kind of thing. And I think it's a pity. There are things I'd have liked to share, especially with my mother.

A chilly gust sweeps over the patio where we're sitting. A cloud passes over Nour's face. Our conversation seems to have revived painful memories. I say nothing. I drink my coffee and wait.

When I was five, one of my cousins touched me. She says this rapidly, without a pause. *I stayed single all through my adolescence. For years, I refused to let any boy go near me. After I left school, I don't really know why, I decided to tell some friends about it. Everything came out. I was so young when it happened, I had no idea. There was never any discussion about that kind of thing in our house. I'd never heard anyone talk about sex. What fondling is, how a woman gets pregnant . . . I had to wait until high school and even then it was only in biology classes, so it was all very cold and scientific.*

Nour is not crying. Nothing in her bearing falters. She has told me her secret and, oddly, she seems strengthened

by it. I realise that, rather than crushing her, this experience has prompted her to make choices that are radical for
a Moroccan woman.

*In Morocco, a woman has no right to feel desire. She may
not choose. But I rebelled. I reject those systems. I don't want
to be like my female cousins who all married very young and
were divorced within two years. I don't want to marry just
anybody, solely in order to appear normal to society. I want
the right to choose. Staying single doesn't worry me. But the
family won't leave me alone. If I could cohabit, I wouldn't
even consider marriage. The problem is not whether it is or
isn't legal, it's whether society will accept it. Other people's
opinions are the most difficult thing. For example, it's legal to
smoke a cigarette but you still can't do it in the street. If you
do, you're called a slut.*

*In my last year of school, I was seeing a boy. It was nice,
but the moment he touched me I froze.* She shudders suddenly. She tries to replay the horror that this physical contact
prompted in her. *It was automatic: as soon as he touched me,
I was horrified. After that I avoided him for years. Until one
day I happened to bump into him and I explained what had
happened. To my great surprise, he was very understanding.
Years later, I fell madly in love with a man. And in the end,
being in love does help.* She starts to laugh, as if to excuse the
naivety she feels she has shown. *There: I was in love, that's all
it took. He knew what he was doing, and I let him do it. And
it went well.*

I was with another man for eight years. From the beginning we agreed we wouldn't think about marriage. We wanted to get to know each other, to have good times together, to share things. This guy was exactly the type of Moroccan man who will never marry a non-virgin. When I met him, he had very old-fashioned ideas about all that. But through our discussions, he started to question a number of things. Now he says he understands that virginity doesn't mean anything. But I think that's just fine words. The pressure of society, parents, religion: all these things come together so that, no matter how much they claim to be open-minded and tolerant, as soon as marriage is on the cards, the girl still has to be a virgin.

Many of the men I've had sexual relationships with have been very selfish. At one point, I even became disgusted with sex itself: I would be giving him pleasure, but it was as if I wasn't there at all. Nour stops and begins to laugh. She pushes her chest out a little. She looks around to check no one is listening, then leans towards me. *You know, one day I decided to be the guy. I said to myself, I'll go to a club, I'll choose the man I want and I'll have him. You see, I needed to do that, and I did it. And it was fantastic! I wanted him. He wanted me. Why should I hold back, what was stopping me? I went for it and it was really good. I have amazing memories from that night.*

At home, we live with another of my father's cousins, who is much older than us and whose parents died young. She's the ultimate virgin, the very model of the frustrated spinster. She thinks it's wrong that I have friends who are men. She tells me: 'You go out and spend time with them, it's natural that they grow tired of you and don't want to marry you.'

And she doesn't even know I'm not a virgin! Sometimes I think that if she were to net a man, it would do her good.

Conservatives and traditionalists: every day, Nour mixes with them in her neighbourhood, in her own family and in her workplace. Her girlfriends haven't always been as sensitive as they might be and she hides her sexual choices from most of them. She protects herself.

Faith – that's between me and my god. I'm a Muslim but I don't practise. Everyone prays in our household. My father is very religious. Since he retired the only place he goes is the mosque. But he doesn't force me to do anything, never asks me why I wear this or don't wear that. It's true that more and more people want to push religion on you. At uni, in our lectures, there were only four out of a hundred girls who didn't wear headscarves. And what I really hate is that these people aren't even religious, it's just a fashion. It's holding us back in lots of ways; it makes interaction harder. At work, for example, I'm the only one who doesn't wear a headscarf. It's mostly men at the office. Once I wore a skirt to work and I felt as if I'd walked in naked. It was awful. I'll never do that again.

Before, my girlfriends and I often used to hold parties in the afternoons, at one of our houses. But at some point that changed. It became a religious gathering where everyone wore hijab and I was constantly being asked why I wasn't wearing it myself. It became a kind of competition, a one-upmanship among the girls over who was the most pious. I won't have anyone push me into that. My mother wears a headscarf; it doesn't bother me. I could decide to wear it one day but that has to come from me.

The other girls, the virgins, they bury their desire deep inside, she says, pushing a hand down hard towards the ground. *They repress it. Like everyone else, I know some girls in hijab who agree to anal sex so as to preserve their hymens. I would choose my own pleasure a thousand times over doing that just so I could stay pure. They don't even think about pleasure; they never address that question.*

Nour made a radical choice. She has gone against the grain of her education and her family, and her lifestyle puts her solidly on the wrong side of the law. *Sometimes, I do have moments of doubt*, she admits to me. *I wonder if I'll never get married because I'm not a virgin. I come from quite a conservative family and I am afraid. I live in a neighbourhood where everyone knows each other and people have nothing better to do than talk to their neighbours and spread nasty rumours. As I'm not a virgin, I could never marry someone I don't already know. Besides, I've told my parents that I'll refuse any proposal from a stranger.*

In the space of an hour, Nour has run the gamut of emotions. At times luminous, at times anxious, I can see that she isn't altogether content in her role of liberated woman. She is making the best of her situation and, as time goes by, she naturally finds her singleness and her life choices ever tougher to bear. *I would like to put a stop to the rumours that do the rounds of the neighbourhood. When you've slept with a man, he always ends up going and boasting to his friends. And then his friends think: 'She's done it with him, why not with me?' They don't understand that I chose him and I don't want anyone else.*

Finally she admits that she is now seeing a man whom she allowed to believe she was a virgin. She doesn't seem to appreciate how degrading this could be. She catches my shocked expression and adds, quite naturally, *I do it as if I had no idea. I give him a crappy time in bed. After all the rumours that went round about me, I was really scared. It's my reputation that's at stake. I don't know, I don't know.* For the first time, she's almost in tears. *Sometimes, I think I'll save up and get my hymen restored. I'm anxious around my parents. I'm afraid of disappointing them. It eats at me. I'm afraid I'll never be married and, more than anything, that I'll never have children. I question my decisions, I wonder if I've made the right choices. Sometimes I even feel like returning to God. You know, I understand those women who choose the veil. I won't do it, because I'm optimistic. But you never know.*

If my father found out, he'd have a heart attack. I could tell my mother, but I don't want to hurt her. Besides, it's so complicated to maintain a sex life: we're always at someone else's place or renting a flat; hotels are impossible. It's miserable: you can never actually carry out this thing which ought to be so simple! I'm not asking for the moon, just to live as I wish, with whoever I wish!

★

Profoundly ambivalent, the Moroccan authorities simultaneously flaunt their ambition to appear modern and

continue to assert that Moroccan society is essentially traditional and clings to bedrock values on all moral questions.
Morocco today is riven with contradictory impulses and
the debates here grow daily more dynamic. We are living
in a kind of cultural chess match in which each party tries
to push its pawns forward, to either rewrite the game or re-
inforce the rules as they are. In this climate, moral matters
and arguments over individual and sexual freedoms are
taking up more and more space in the media and whipping
up public opinion on all sides.

The debate around abortion that took place at the beginning of 2015 is, as such, rather revealing of the tentative
advances in this domain. Up to that point, article 449 of the
penal code provided for punishment of between one and
five years in prison and a fine of 200–500 dirhams (18–46
euros) for any person having provoked or attempted to pro-
voke an abortion with or without the consent of the party
concerned. Article 454 punished any woman having carried out a termination upon herself with a prison term of
between six months and two years. And finally, article 455
prescribed terms of between two months and two years for
all accomplices to an abortion, notably all intermediaries or
vendors of products for abortions. According to AMLAC,
Morocco's charity against clandestine abortion, nearly six
hundred secret abortions are carried out every day and
hundreds of women die as a result of the appalling medical

conditions. For years, doctors and activists have been fighting to bring these horrifying statistics to light. The principal figurehead for this struggle, Dr Chafik Chraïbi, has made a major contribution to the publicity around this societal problem, to the point of forcing legislators to undertake a thorough review.

Under the leadership of King Mohammed VI, doctors, psychiatrists, religious leaders, charity campaigners and the relevant government ministers met over January and February of 2015 to discuss the problem, 'in the context of Islamic law'. Despite the hopes fostered by this discussion, the legal framework for voluntary termination of pregnancy was broadened only to include cases of rape, incest and severe foetal abnormalities. 'That debate was a powerful and emotional moment, an occasion for different factions in Moroccan society to express their positions, to describe some of their personal experiences, and also a moment when we were able to see that our different positions weren't as clear-cut as we all thought', explains psychiatrist Jalil Bennani, who took an active part in the discussions. 'Some modernisers turned out to be more hesitant. Some hard-line Islamists were broadly keen on a degree of reform. Some women were anti, while some of the men were strongly in favour of reform. It was, I feel, an important occasion.'

In fact, the debate was so focused on health questions that issues of sexual freedom and women's rights over their own bodies were completely ignored. As Dr Chraïbi commented in an interview for *Jeune Afrique*: 'Moroccan society is profoundly divided: we say we want to modernise and to protect our people, but the issue of sex is still taboo. We have to talk about it. It isn't a solely medical problem. Badly handled abortions, septicaemia, infections, suicides, honour crimes, abandoned babies and infanticides represent real problems for Moroccan society, problems we must solve once and for all.' You could of course argue that it should in any case be impossible to legalise abortion in a country where sexual relations outside marriage are illegal. It would amount to saying that a woman might legally terminate her pregnancy but should then be arrested if the child was conceived outside wedlock.

In the summer of 2015, I was able to meet Mona Eltahawy, an Egyptian feminist and author of the excellent book *Headscarves and Hymens: Why the Middle East Needs a Sexual Revolution*. We talked passionately for hours. I told her about my conversations with Moroccan women and of my wish to share these testimonies, but also of my fury when I realised that these women were forever havering between the freedom they desired and the shackles forced upon them. Why, for example, were so many of them considering hymen restoration surgery or wearing a headscarf when they had expressly freed themselves from such conventions? How to explain these backward steps, these resurgences of guilt? Eltahawy responded by reminding me of words famously attributed to Harriet Tubman, the great American abolitionist who devoted her life to persuading slaves to flee the plantations and claim their freedom. She is meant to have said: 'I freed a thousand slaves. I could have freed a thousand more if only they knew they were slaves.' Emancipation, Eltahawy told me, is first about raising awareness. If women haven't fully understood the state of inferiority in which they are kept, they will do nothing but perpetuate it.

We talked too about the strength of our taboos and we agreed on one key point: the Arab revolutions, the emergence of the middle classes and the arrival of online social networks have indeed helped to loosen, somewhat, that stranglehold of silence. In Morocco, since King Mohammed VI's accession in 1999, we have seen much greater freedom of speech. In the media, on the social networks, in the press and even in the streets, we can now address questions relating to morality, sexual freedom and abortion. Of course, public opinion remains deeply divided and the climate broadly tends towards the traditionalists, but at least we're talking about the issues that affect us. News stories that, only a short time ago, would have been passed over in silence are now discussed and argued over in the media and at the heart of public life.

For some publications, features on sex have become standard, even indispensable. In the 1990s, the women's magazine *Femmes du Maroc* forged a reputation with its famous 'black pages', in which journalists addressed sexual themes. Today there are numerous weeklies that devote their headline articles to subjects such as homosexuality, Moroccans' sexual fulfilment, pornography, etc. As everywhere else in the world,

sex sells papers and brings readers in droves. Our privately
owned media platforms, which began to emerge alongside Morocco's state media in 2005, have taken this truism
to heart. Independent radio stations such as Hit Radio are
offering more and more programmes on sexual subjects (see
'Faty Badi: "Our society is still very prudish and conservative,
and . . . totally obsessed with sex"', p. 53). In 2017, the television network 2M began broadcasting *Love Through the Eyes
of . . .*, a series of documentaries made by ten great Moroccan
directors (including Sonia Terrab, Laïla Marrakchi and
Narjiss Nejjar, among others). Focusing on the role of love in
our society, this innovative programme seduced the nation.
On 3 April 2017, the film directed by Laïla Marrakchi and
produced by Nabil Ayouch was watched by nearly 2 million
people – and provoked some outraged responses online. 2M
was accused of broadcasting a 'shameful' and 'pornographic'
programme importing 'western values that are foreign to
our culture'. And the subject of this furore? A sequence in
which young people speak very freely about their feelings
about love and sex outside marriage. One young woman,
speaking straight to camera, very courageously lambasts
society's hypocritical attitude to women and denounces
the sacrosanct status of virginity. In the end 2M defended
its programme as exploring 'the societal reality' of Morocco.
And Marrakchi, the director, concluded coyly that 'talking
about love and sex in Morocco remains very challenging'.

Moroccan society is still quite prudish about all these issues. I remember that in my childhood, watching television or at the cinema, we often struggled to understand a film's plot because all the sex scenes and even the kisses had been edited out. But it would be unfair to say that Moroccan society is intrinsically puritan: affection, seduction and humour are all valued highly in popular culture. Nonetheless, over the last thirty years, the influence of Wahhabism, a soulless Islam, has undermined our *hanane*, the tenderness which constituted one of the pillars of popular culture for Fatima Mernissi.

In November 2014, a survey carried out by the weekly magazine *TelQuel* demonstrated how conservative Moroccan society really is on questions relating to sex: 84% are against sexual freedom, 83% are against tolerance for homosexuality – and the women are even more conservative than the men, for 90% of women interviewed were against sexual freedom while 'only' 78% of the men shared that view.

In Morocco, it is unthinkable to kiss someone on the mouth in the street or to display affection in public. I must have been about ten the first time I went to Paris, and I still remember being literally rooted to the spot in amazement at a couple who were kissing in the middle of the street, indifferent to passers-by who, in any case, didn't so much as glance at them. In Morocco this was absolutely unimaginable, not to mention potentially dangerous. Yet this is what two teenagers from Nador, a town of conservative reputation in the north-east of the kingdom, attempted to do. In 2013, a boy and a girl, fifteen and four-teen years old respectively, posted a photo on Facebook of themselves kissing. Following a complaint lodged by a local NGO, they were arrested along with the friend who had taken the photo and prosecuted for 'breach of modesty' and 'publication of compromising images'. They were held for three days in a centre for minors in Nador. Their arrest immediately roused the social networks where, in deliberate rebellion, a large number of young people began posting photos of their own kisses. The Alternative Movement for Personal Freedoms (MALI), along with other campaigns that had grown out of the so-called 20 February Movement, which was born in the wake of the Tunisian and Egyptian Spring uprisings, even organised a 'kiss-in' in front of the Parliament building in Rabat. Under popular pressure, the judiciary authorities in Nador were obliged to let the three teenagers go.

But the news story that has unquestionably prompted the most ink to be spilled is the case of Amina El-Filali. In March 2012, this sixteen-year-old girl committed suicide in Larache, near Tangier, by swallowing rat poison. Having been raped by a family friend, she was forced to marry her rapist in an arrangement between her family and that of the criminal. Public outcry then brought to light the penal code's scandalous article 475, under which a rapist who marries his victim may no longer be liable for his crime.

According to this law, the corruption of a minor is punishable by imprisonment of between one and five years plus a fine of 200–500 dirhams. But it was the remainder of the article that caused the uproar. 'When a marriageable minor thus abducted or corrupted has married her rapist, the latter may not be prosecuted except following accusation by those people qualified to request annulment of the marriage, and may not be sentenced until after such annulment of the marriage has been confirmed.' To the archaism of this Moroccan statute was added the inhumanity of certain official responses, notably that of the female Islamist minister for family and social cohesion, Bassima Hakkaoui, who dusted off the well-worn argument of western interference in justification: 'Article 475 of the penal code runs no risk of being repealed from one day to the next due to the pressure of international opinion. Often the marriage of a rape subject to her rapist does not cause her any real harm.'

'Often the marriage of a rape subject to her rapist does not cause her any real harm.'

Demonstrations were organised. Women waved portraits of the young dead girl and registered their rejection of the condition of Moroccan women. On social networks, the case ignited public opinion. This mobilisation of civil society was not in vain: two years after El-Filali's suicide, the offending paragraph was repealed by parliament.

These days, some militant feminists and defenders of personal rights dare to campaign publicly for the repeal of article 490, which forbids sexual relations outside marriage. Some heirs to the 20 February Movement have put the legalisation of sexual relationships squarely on their agendas. Founded in 2009 by Zineb El-Rhazaoui and Ibtissame Lachgar, MALI fights tirelessly on this front and on that of rights for homosexuals. Khadija Ryadi, president of the Moroccan Association for Human Rights (AMDH), likewise condemns the state's hypocrisy: 'We know that sexual relationships outside wedlock are common in Morocco. The fact that all of them must be hidden only promotes abuse and attacks on personal freedoms.'

The former minister for family and social cohesion, Nouzha Skalli, bravely spoke out against the retention of the article and against our leaders' hypocrisy: 'The social reality, which we cannot ignore, runs in complete contradiction to that article: in order to apply the law, we would have to build dozens of new prisons to house thousands of people.' For the lawyer Youssef Chehbi, who has defended several homosexuals and was film director Nabil Ayouch's counsel over the *Much Loved* case (see 'Society on the Verge of a Nervous Breakdown', p. 57): 'We are living in a system that turns us all into outlaws and therefore we are afraid and we don't take action. Our main concern is always how not to get caught!' For Chehbi, this is about neither morality nor religion. 'Morality always means other people's morals, as Léo Ferré said. And anyway, morality and the law are two quite separate things.

Today, we could do with clarifying the difference. We are a bastard generation: having inherited an archaic system, we are, at the same time, living through an extraordinary technological revolution. In less than fifty years, we have been parachuted out of the Stone Age and into modernity. Now, the only way to fight those outdated ties and the misogyny, homophobia, etc. that they promote is to educate our youth and, above all, to face up to our contradictions.'

On the other side, the Islamists are entrenching their positions. 'Any sexual act whatsoever outside marriage is considered an act of debauchery, a crime,' stated MP Abouzaid El Mokri. 'Have these permissive philosophies that come from Europe improved social and family relationships in that continent? I think not.'

At the *Economist*'s forum of 29 June 2015, on being questioned about the potential legalisation of sexual relationships outside marriage, the Islamist justice minister Mustapha Ramid replied: 'If they are legalised, I will resign. In any case, we're not about to start going into couples' houses. If the neighbours don't lodge a complaint with the authorities because an unmarried couple is disturbing them, the latter will never be brought to justice.' This is the bizarre conceit of a justice ministry that allows the application of its law to depend upon neighbourly tale-telling and the local grapevine. Among traditionalists, as in a large swathe of Moroccan society, the notion of an impenetrable barrier between public and private spaces has become entrenched. Hence the infamous hadith that goes 'If you fall into temptation, do it discreetly': one way of admitting the natural, human roles played by temptation and sexual relationships outside marriage – which are admissible as long as everything takes place in private. This is the argument trumpeted by Islamists in the debates about homosexuality: we refuse to tolerate or accept homosexuality, but we will not seek to discover whatever goes on behind the bedroom door. This explains why Morocco's Islamist Justice and Development Party (PJD) condemned an attack on a homosexual couple inside a house in Beni Mellal. The reasoning is false; nonetheless I can't help pointing out that it's a new development for a justice minister and an Islamist prime minister to address questions of sex outside marriage and even of homosexuality without lapsing into hate-filled diatribes.

Because discussion of these topics is generally very tense indeed. In June 2012, during a programme on the satellite network Al Mayadeen, Mokhtar Laghzioui, chief editor of Moroccan daily paper *Al Ahdath Al Maghribia*, showed extraordinary courage when he spoke out in favour of sexual freedom. 'Do you really mean complete sexual freedom?' shot back journalist Lina Zahreddine. 'Even if it was your mother or your sister, or your wife?'

'They have the right to do as they wish with their own bodies,' Laghzioui replied.

Extremist cleric Abdellah Nhari, who is well known for his violent outbursts, required no further prompt to call for the editor's assassination, calling him a traitor and a cuckold. As another journalist, Sanaa El Aji, pointed out to me, if it had been a woman defending the sexual freedom of her son or brother, doubtless there would have been no such outcry ... For when we talk about sexual freedom, men's dominance naturally creates a very unlevel playing field indeed.

In August 2016 came an event that threw a spotlight on every problematic aspect of the sexual legislation that we have been looking at: social hypocrisy, the insecurity caused by arbitrary application of the law, and the yawning gulf between public discourse and private morality. The situation is almost too perfect an illustration of our leaders' pious yet hollow grandstanding.

The scene occurs at dawn, near a beach in Mohammedia, inside an old Mercedes. The protagonists: Fatima Nejjar, sixty-two, and Moulay Omar Benhammad, sixty-three. Discovered in 'a sexual position' by the police, they are arrested 'in the act of adultery'. This scene, versions of which take place every day in Morocco and other North African countries, is particularly delightful because of the nature of the two protagonists, both of them being respected figures in the dogmatic branch of Morocco's governing PJD.

Fatima Nejjar typically sports a closely pinned headscarf and, in the images broadcast on TV, an austere expression, the very image of seriousness. A widow, she is known for her highly conservative rallying speeches. In one video, we can watch her warning young women against lust and explaining to them that women's gaze and laughter are an incitement to fornication. A professor of Islamic studies, Moulay Omar Benhammad is married and, since 2013, primarily known for having issued a fatwa banning the exchange of love letters on Facebook.

The two lovers have, then, formed the vanguard of the struggle against vice and depravity. They figure among those who feed a morbid puritanism into Moroccan society, spluttering about fornication and homosexuals, attacking women's liberty and music festivals. As often happens to the devout, they're obsessed with sex and, with the assurance of those who haven't committed a single sin, they threaten filthy sinners with hell, and pave the way for further misogyny and hatred.

Naturally, their case opened the floodgates. The public took ample opportunity to mock the pair of hypocrites. More conservative adherents sought sheepishly to excuse the lovers. But we would be wrong to ignore the tragedy obscured by this farce. For what Nejjar and Benhammad experienced is what dozens of Moroccans live through every day, and no attention is paid to *them*. This pair of Islamists experienced for themselves the randomness and the humiliations of the system. They were obliged to recognise that exposure of a person's most private sexual practice is a deadly weapon in the hands of those who wish to take control of them or carry out personal revenge. Eventually, the Forum for the Respect of Human Rights, a charity close to the PJD, would even publish a press release asserting that 'the application of articles 490, 491 and 492 of the penal code by government employees responsible for applying these laws may undermine individuals' freedoms and citizens' constitutional rights. Furthermore, such misapplication of the laws exposes citizens to degrading and inhuman treatment, which compromises their dignity.'

Sordid extracts from the case report were leaked to the press, which went to town on questions of used paper tissues, semen and other grubby details . . . You can't help feeling a twinge of sympathy at this pathetic situation in which two sexagenarians were reduced to hiding in a car in order to snatch a moment's intimacy. Entirely against their will, they became Morocco's figureheads for sexual deprivation.

ZHOR

'LIBERATE SEX!'

Zhor and I first got in contact online. I was in Morocco to talk about my novel and she had heard about my work. I had also heard of her, through a mutual friend. We agreed to meet in Rabat, outside the train station. From the platform, I saw a young woman arrive dressed in the latest fashion, her hair cut very short. She had an air of great self-assurance. The way she moved, how she spoke to people, everything about her, suggested that she had fought hard to achieve her place in the world. And that she was determined to be respected. We sat beneath trees in the garden of a small hotel close to the station.

Zhor is not the type to waste time with small talk. She prefers to get straight to the point.

I'm twenty-eight and single, she said. *It suits me very well and I have no intention of marrying. Or rather, I might; I might if it suited me. Marriage is a business deal like any other, isn't it?* I am a little shocked by her lack of romanticism, and by the somewhat provocative way she is talking about men. She backtracks. *I have been in love in the past, it's true. But I would want to live with the person first, be free to shape the partnership I want. That's why I absolutely have to leave this country. I'm sick of pissing in the wind. I'd rather get out.*

Zhor comes from a poor background. She has four sisters and a brother. Now retired, her father used to work as caretaker at a corporate office. Her mother has never worked; she brought up the children.

My father was ultra-conservative. Once, when I was at secondary school, I plucked my eyebrows. He was in the middle of praying but he stopped and said: 'You shall grow them back. I feel like I'm looking at a whore!' I even remember this ridiculous time when he got angry because two of my teddies were cuddling in a way he felt was immodest. Saying that, I know they weren't always so conservative. My father only began to say daily prayers when he was forty-three.

My mother covers her hair because my father makes her. She's a very submissive wife. I've always thought of her as a victim. She married my father at sixteen to escape from her brother, who was extremely violent. It was my father who told her to wear a headscarf, to put trousers under her djellaba, to stop wearing make-up, even moisturiser.

All through my childhood, they told me over and over that sleeping with people was wrong, but that never really stuck in my head. And as luck would have it, my first time was a rape, by three men, when I was fifteen. I was on my way from school to my evening class. The first man made me go into a room. He locked me in. I didn't understand at all. Another guy came in and he raped me. I was a virgin and there was some blood, which surprised him, I think. For them, I was a whore. The third one finished off the job. I stood up and got dressed. I caught the bus and went back home. At the time, I think I was more afraid of my parents and everyone else than about the rape itself. I thought they were going to lock me up,

*that they'd accuse me of having encouraged the men. I told
my friends at school and word went round. It was awful for
my reputation in the neighbourhood.*

*Rape is very common, especially among girls who already
have active sex lives. Men don't understand the difference
between having a sex life and consenting to a single sexual
act. Besides, what tips it in their favour is that they know the
girls will never report them.*

*Three years later, I slept with someone without knowing
how you do it. I did it just like that, without a thought, automatically. No man had taught me how to enjoy myself or to
understand my body. At eighteen I realised what the clitoris
was. I was with a boy who didn't want to put on a condom. So
I wouldn't let him penetrate me. We touched each other instead,
and that was when I found I had something that could give me
pleasure. I went home and for a week I did nothing but masturbate. I felt like I'd made the discovery of the century: this
free thing that you could do without anyone else.*

It's hard to know what Zhor really thinks. She enjoys being
shocking, using the same tone to talk about her rape as
about her discovery of the joys of masturbation. I'm sure
there's an element of game-playing in all this. That she is
protecting herself from others' judgement by shouting from
the rooftops that she doesn't care. I know too that whatever
force thrusts a woman out of conventional paths must be
so violent that she will naturally reflect that violence back

upon others. At least Zhor has had one piece of luck. She has grown up surrounded by sisters to whom she seems very close and with whom she has shared almost everything.

My sisters and I used to run wild. When the satellite dishes started popping up around the neighbourhood, we began watching porn films on the American networks. I used to keep watch to make sure our parents never caught us. Then we started spending hours watching British entertainment channel Venus TV on satellite. We would watch it at five o'clock while drinking tea with our mother. She had left school very young, she didn't know anything. For her, sex was so taboo that she must have thought: 'I'll let them learn from elsewhere all that I was never taught.' We never talked about sex with her, not even about contraception. Besides, she didn't know the first thing! One day I had to explain to her that the pill has to be taken every day, you can't just take it when you want. If she had known before, perhaps she wouldn't have had so many children.

My parents are very hung up on virginity. When my sisters were married, their husbands' families demanded virginity certificates which my father was proud to produce for them. So my sister had to explain what they were to me. She drew it in cartoon pictures, she told me the whole story.

When I ask Zhor how a young woman like her goes about freeing herself from a family world like this, she begins to laugh. *You know, I was reading a lot. Actually, there's one*

thing I do owe my father: every Saturday he took me to bor-
row library books. I often used to choose books about anat-
omy, about the human body. He thought I would become a
doctor so he liked that. He always let me choose the ones I
wanted. And my parents also realised that I was unshakeable
over certain things. However conservative they are, they're
intelligent people. No one ever made me pray. My father categorically refuses to let me wear the veil because he thinks it
would hold me back in my career.

I was at a girls' secondary school where we talked about sex
all the time. There was a lot of porn around. In our working-class
neighbourhood, the girls used to go out with the local big guns.
Guys who were fresh out of prison and who had swagger. At
uni, I spent the first year living in student
accommodation. It was very educational.
I realised that everyone, and I mean
everyone, was fucking. Even the girls who
were veiled head to toe had their sex lives.
The key thing was to be discreet. In public,
the girls will always deny it. I didn't meet
many with campaigning instincts. Most
of them live double lives, depending on whether they're with
their families or their friends. They make it work as best they
can.

> 'I realised that everyone, and I mean everyone, was fucking. Even the girls who were veiled head to toe.'

At uni, it seemed to me that sex almost always involved
exploitation. The girls who wore hijab would sleep with someone in the hope of marriage. Others were in prostitution to pay
for their studies and their clothes. In the room next to mine

there were three of them. They accepted it completely. At night they were able to leave the student compound thanks to the night guard, who was in on the scheme. On weekends, when their parents came to collect them, they would put their head-scarves and their ankle-length coats back on. I remember they used some truly antiquated methods for protecting themselves from diseases, old wives' remedies that did nothing at all. In any case, the STD that Moroccans are most afraid of is babies.

Zhor seems genuinely to speak for those of the younger generation of Moroccans who have come to terms with the pervasive double standards. Like many her age, she adapts to the different circumstances and social circles that she moves between. More than anything, she knows that she's part of one of the first generations of women to experience true social mobility, living alone in a big city and making their own choice of partner. A way of life that is, all considered, completely new to the country.

My generation grew up with the internet. So I get the feeling that we've rather forgotten what's going on around us, in our own neighbourhoods, in our country. Our lives are virtual. Anyway, what's clear is that sex is not a luxury. Whatever their personal income, people want to have sex. When I think again about that business of the kids from Nador on Facebook, I think the problem is not that we're conservative but that we're fucked up. Love and affection are as taboo as sex. One day, I was watching a film and I started to laugh: 'The boy is in love with the girl!' My father slapped me and said it's vulgar to say that. I grew up with the idea that love leads

automatically to sex and that every demonstration of love is
about sex. My parents never made a single loving gesture.

For Zhor, not pushing our legislation forward is a political
choice more than a moral or religious one. *We are keeping*
people frustrated. That way, their primary concern is how and
with whom they'll get a screw instead of starting a revolution
over their living conditions. Walking my dog this morning, I
saw a guy come out of a sewer where he'd been sleeping. In
the neighbourhood I grew up in, when the price of semolina
increases by one dirham, the women have to give up their
Friday couscous. We live surrounded by vast poverty and we
don't rebel. The simple task of finding somewhere to make
love requires an incredible degree of planning. Before, with
my guy, we used to end up in the toilets. We hadn't the money
to rent an apartment or hotel rooms. One day at the beach, a
cop came by just as I was kissing my boyfriend. He began to
insult me. He asked if my father knew what I was doing. I told
him my father didn't care and that he could take me to the
police station if he wanted. I knew that the problem would be
solved by a hundred dirhams. It was stupid.

For lots of men, a woman is no more than a vagina in
which you masturbate. Girls are very crude, very street
when they talk about sex. We talk a lot more directly about
it than boys do. We give each other warnings, we suggest
smart approaches. We support each other. It should be said
that men benefit hugely from the situation and that the great
majority of them still don't back women's independence. At

uni, the director of student affairs asked me why I was smoking outside. For him it was an affront, yet at the same time the boys were smoking joints inside the halls of residence, in front of everyone. What drives me wild is that there are whole chapters of the penal code about morality, but all they talk about is women.

The mere process of looking for an apartment as a solo woman is like negotiating an assault course. My parents had no problem with me living alone. From the moment I started to earn a salary, I stopped asking their advice. But it took me three months to find a landlord who would rent to a single woman. Each time they would come up with some excuse. In fact, they're just afraid of local gossip. They think a single woman will bring men back or open a brothel. I was even asked for written authorisation from my father. Yet I earn twice as much as my father – it's ridiculous!

In this country, you can't wear what you want, even though there are advertising posters everywhere showing girls who are half-naked. In the real world, you don't go out after 9 p.m. The street isn't for you. You are always an intruder in public spaces. People do talk a lot about sex on the radio and in women's magazines, but it's always within the legal constraints: certain things are discussed but we all know the boundaries.

These days, there are a few charities and some activists who dare to tackle these subjects. Some movements even talk about gay liberation. But let's liberate sex first!

FATY BADI

'OUR SOCIETY IS STILL VERY PRUDISH AND CONSERVATIVE, AND . . . TOTALLY OBSESSED WITH SEX'

In 2012, alongside sexologist Doc Samad, Faty Badi presented a Sunday call-in show on Hit Radio. *On t'écoute – We're Listening to You –* was a weekly magazine-format show broadcast from 10 p.m. to midnight. Badi received calls, emails and text messages from young listeners around the country hoping to share their worries and to receive advice. I wanted to meet her.

The listeners all had one thing in common: a fundamental ignorance about their bodies, especially when it came to sexual practices. Young Moroccan men live in a genuine Catch-22. They are encouraged to begin their sex lives very early, but at the same time no one explains how they should go about it. There is no sex education in our school system, hence the widespread anxiety about sex among our young people.

I soon realised that our programme had a real pedagogical purpose. But the scale of the work to be done was completely overwhelming. I allowed myself to be consumed by the job and by all the stories, many of them tragic, that I was privileged to hear. In Morocco, people aren't used to speaking up in public. So when they call, it's like the floodgates open, no filter at all. We were receiving up to three thousand calls per evening! Some of them told us in detail about their STDs.

Others described rapes, assaults or marriages they'd been forced into. They expected us to come up with solutions for them, which was often simply impossible.

My worst call was from a girl from Kenitra who was barely thirteen. She told us that her father had married her to one of his friends. They had lied to the judge about her age in order to finalise the marriage. This little girl said to us: 'I want to go to secondary school and play with my friends. Can you call my husband? I know that he sees women his own age, sometimes he even brings them home. I watch porn. I would really like to satisfy him but he doesn't want to touch me.' That floored me. We used to get a lot of calls like that from the small towns, where people have nothing better to do.

> **'I want to go to secondary school and play with my friends. Can you call my husband?'**

Thanks to Facebook, younger people don't have the same relationship with what's forbidden or taboo. The independent radio stations have also played their part in freeing up what we can talk about. When you listen carefully, you realise that young people's attitudes to sex can actually be quite uninhibited. Sometimes we even have to impose our own boundaries on them. It's been staggering to see the taboos melt away like this. One father called us to say that his daughter wasn't very fulfilled in her sex life and he wanted to offer her some advice.

There was also a lot of sexual violence, calls from women who'd been beaten or raped. Audience figures rocketed and there was clearly an element of voyeurism among those who were listening to us. Across the media, sex has become a *business. There are even religious programmes with dodgy imams giving advice. Herbal pharmacists and other charlatans have cottoned on to the racket. Our society is still very prudish and conservative, and yet, at the same time, we're totally obsessed with sex and sexual performance. The population is suffering from a genuine case of split personality. Moroccans are huge consumers of pornography but also keen users of dating websites and dirty-talk platforms. Even so, their understanding of sex is very naive, even among married couples. I've talked to women who, though well educated, had never seen a gynaecologist and thought they could catch Aids from a soft drink.*

What makes me despair is the apathy among our reformers. They don't want to give up their comforts and privileges. No one will rock the boat. There are fundamentalist upsurges that we're unable to respond to. Nothing holds the extremists back: they have both absolute conviction and enormous energy. When I see those people demonstrating outside a homosexual person's house or indeed that lawyer with his lawsuit against Jennifer Lopez, I am appalled (see the next chapter: 'Society on the Verge of a Nervous Breakdown'). And then we have a very difficult relationship with the West, which we see as both a model and an evil bogeyman. I believe we have a serious inferiority complex when it comes to our views on Europe.

All this sexual frustration leads to violent and vicious social interactions. When everyone is lying and faking, sexual relationships become a way of exercising control over people.

For example, having come to the end of a relationship, some contemptible men will share a young woman's most intimate information, they will publicly humiliate her and wreck her reputation. Nor is it rare for women to betray each other or threaten each other's reputations. Girls are forced to act holier-than-thou and so they end up living in a web of lies. How many times have I met a woman who wears hijab and acts very modestly, only to find out she's some married man's mistress?

The feminist struggle our mothers were fighting has lost momentum and we haven't yet taken up the baton. We absolutely have to challenge the laws and bring down the whole legislative regime. We should be telling the truth about it all. The problem is that we're always on the wrong side of the law. If someone bears a grudge against me, they will always have a way of attacking me and having me arrested. Our moral system forces us to live in legal grey areas. This means we can never pursue our cause all the way – because we're afraid to.

SOCIETY ON THE VERGE OF A NERVOUS BREAKDOWN

THE CRAZY SUMMER OF 2015

Premiered at the 2015 Directors' Fortnight, the independent parallel to the formal Cannes Film Festival, Nabil Ayouch's film *Much Loved* triggered an intensely aggressive reaction in Morocco. Merely broadcasting a few stills from this story of four prostitute friends in Marrakesh proved enough to unleash the fury of the masses, followed by that of the authorities. The film, its director and actors received insults and death threats. Without even having seen the film, the minister for culture and press decided to ban it. His intention: to protect the virtuous – and completely unrealistic – image of the Moroccan woman, which Ayouch's film would have undermined. In Morocco, when someone holds a mirror up to you, you smash the glass.

A week after the furore began, I went to meet Nabil Ayouch. Despite the vitriol he had been facing, he was very calm and poised. We chatted in his office, in a working-class part of Casablanca.

When you see a woman as a machine for procreation, a thing that isn't meant to feel pleasure, and when her body is practically your own property, how are you meant to have a healthy approach to sex? Moroccan men are repressed,

they're frustrated. Everything that has to do with our appe-
tites, our desires, is rejected because we've taught ourselves to
demonise all that.

So when we make people confront this image of themselves,
their reaction is extreme and violent. I believe that what people
have seen in my film has hurt them. They've had to face their
own frustrations. Every day they're required to play a role, and
in the end they can't stand to have their mask pulled off.

Of course, prostitution as a subject is very taboo. But I think
what's shocked people most is the social aspect of this activity,
the fact that thousands of families make their living from it.
Thousands of prostitutes are their family's breadwinner, yet
we go on seeing them as pariahs. They are rejected, mocked,
hidden away. We are at an impasse. We cover ourselves in
false virtue even while, by forbidding sexual relationships
outside marriage, our system promotes the commercialisa-
tion of the body, and especially violence to and exploitation
of the female body.

Sex has become the latest red line. Moroccans swing between
fantasy and vilification. We are the fifth-biggest consumer of
internet porn in the world, yet at the same time we're constantly calling for modesty. Some 160,000 people went to see
Jennifer Lopez, 1.5 million Moroccans watched that concert
on television, and now they insult her online because she was
dressed too provocatively. These days, we're confronted with our
own conflicting identities: sex is associated with the Other, the
decadent West, while Moroccan and Muslim identity stands
for virtue and modesty. But we're forgetting everything. We're

forgetting that it's we Arabs, we Muslims, who shocked the West with our erotic texts in the fifteenth century. We invented the realm of the erotic. We're suffering from collective amnesia.

I decided to showcase a 'reverse anthropology': my characters are prostitutes, of course, but they've also taken control of their lives. The men are practically supporting characters, emasculated, in the women's service. What upset people, what shocked viewers particularly, was the fact that men could be merely peripheral figures. Men's masculinity is undermined and that's why they respond with such hatred.

In order to write this film, Ayouch carried out extensive interviews. For nearly a year and a half, he met with hundreds of prostitutes who told him their stories. He talked to girls who offer sex to building-site labourers and receive payment in vegetables. He met others who rake in 100,000 dirhams for a single night and are driven around in luxury limos.

They described barbarous scenes to me, appalling humiliations. The overall picture is absolutely miserable, perverted and vile. I was horribly shocked. I felt deep sadness for these women. These days, sex is everywhere: it has filtered into our homes on television, with social networks and through porn. And yet it seems to me that our deep conservativism means this sex can't be appreciated in a healthy way. These days, a mere sentence, a word, a skirt that's too short, will cause a scandal. We keep pushing for more virtuous female models. These are backward steps. What's more, the social networks act as a powerful megaphone for the most conservative and frustrated voices among us.

During the controversy over my film, the women's charities were notable for their silence, yet their own daughters', their children's, futures are at stake. For too long, women's charities have avoided tackling issues that are clearly to do with sex. They're scared of being accused of perverting Moroccan society and they've ended up abandoning this crucial aspect of the field.

Our cult of purity is abusive. We set women up on a completely artificial pedestal, we treat them like precious stones that must be protected from the malicious gaze of men. But in the end, what does this mean for men's own self-image?

That evening, I met another director, Noureddine Lakhmari, who had instantly leapt to Ayouch's defence in the media and on social networks. Moroccans know Lakhmari as the person who put Casablanca on the map as a hub for contemporary cinema. In *Casanegra* he filmed the underworld of our 'white city', the sordid bars and the prostitution. He told stories of love on the edge; he brought us images of sex that was violent, hidden and shameful. *In my view, the problem is that we don't talk about love. In Morocco, people are afraid of beauty, afraid of affection. All day long we watch videos of Daesh, including live assassinations, yet we can't stand to watch a kiss on television. Our understanding of what is pornographic is quite*

'All day long we watch videos of Daesh, including live assassinations, yet we can't stand to watch a kiss on television.'

weird. We can't accept a film like Much Loved *even though everyone knows that this is exactly what our society is like.*

For the writer Sonia Terrab (author of *Shamablanca* and *La Révolution n'a pas eu lieu* – 'The Revolution Didn't Happen' – and director of the superb television documentary *Shakespeare in Casablanca*): *There is a sexual revolution, but it's happening underground. We just have to bring it out, into daylight. Here we are free only inside locked rooms. We pay for our freedom, to be able to drink in peace and dress as we wish.*

That summer, I was in Rabat for a relaxed family holiday. Everyone was talking about the *Much Loved* affair. Some were indignant at the criticism the film had attracted. Others felt that Morocco was not obliged to license the distribution of a pornographic film, one that undermined the country's image. In taxis and cafes, on the tram and at elegant dinner parties, I sometimes struggled to keep my cool when confronted with opinions from people the great majority of whom had not actually seen the film.

The Mawazine music festival, which is held annually in Rabat and attracts hundreds of thousands, ought to have taken our minds off things. But that year, it seemed instead to stoke the flames. This festival has always been a prime target for Islamists. They accuse it not only of being too costly but also of inviting decadent artists who have a calamitous effect on young people's morals. In 2010, Mustapha

Ramid, then president of the PJD, the Islamist parliamen-
tary party, opposed Elton John's invitation, which he considered an 'encouragement of homosexuality in Morocco'.
The party's official newspaper, *Attajdid*, even talked about
a plot to 'homosexualise' the country. John did eventually
perform, to the great delight of his audience. The next year,
Bassima Hakkaoui, at the time a PJD member of parliament,
launched an attack on the Colombian singer Shakira, whose
show she considered 'pornographic'.

In that summer of 2015, it was the American star Jennifer
Lopez's appearance that triggered the controversy. On
stage the singer wore a leotard and was surrounded by
female dancers themselves substantially exposed and
whose hip thrusts were very suggestive. In the hours that
followed the broadcast on the 2M television network, the
social networks were inundated by criticism of the show's
pornographic nature. The minister for communication,
Mustapha El Khalfi, ended up producing a press release in
which he stated that 'what was broadcast was unacceptable
and contravened the laws on radio broadcasting'.

Even worse, an allegation of infringement of modesty
was lodged against the star, by an unknown plaintiff. They
accused her of having 'danced and sung songs of undeni-
able depravity and bad taste, using suggestive movements
and poses prejudicial to modesty and morality. All this in
the presence of an audience largely made up of minors.' On

5 June, almost one hundred and fifty members of the PJD's youth movement demonstrated outside Parliament. The name Jennifer Lopez was on everyone's lips. Anonymous callers demanded that Morocco expel this instrument of Satan and purveyor of lewdness. As for me, I was horrified. I was shocked to hear middle-class people, normally proud liberals, saying: 'She's free to do that in her own country. Here we don't behave like whores.'

A few days later, I struck up a conversation with Rachid, a man who works in my neighbourhood, mostly looking after gardens. He's a softly spoken man, very polite, who has always talked very humbly with me. I know he is married and has a young daughter and that he lives very modestly by cobbling together odd jobs. He never talks about religion and displays no outward sign of piety.

We fall to talking about the festival and the overcharged atmosphere of the last few days. At this, to my great surprise, Rachid loses his temper. *If I had known*, he says, *I would have gone there with friends and we would have slashed her, that whore. How shameful it is to see such things in our country! She can do that stuff back home. Why does she come here provoking Muslims in their own country?*

A few days later, it's the band Placebo that's making the headlines. The singer has come on stage with a crossed-through number 489 on his chest, in protest against the clause penalising homosexuality. The conservatives are on the verge of meltdown. 'Who *are* these foreign artists who feel they can come here and preach to us in our own country?' they chorus in the media. This is the moment that two activists from the radical Ukrainian feminist group FEMEN choose to stage a topless kiss on the esplanade that runs up to the Hassan Tower, in the heart of Rabat. They are arrested and expelled from Morocco in a matter of hours.

In this poisonous and highly volatile atmosphere, the craziest rumours begin going around. According to the gossip, two young men from a poor neighbourhood are hoping to recreate the FEMEN intervention. In response, a group of about twenty people decide to demonstrate outside the young men's home, shouting 'No homosexuals here' and 'Save Islam'. They come from the charity Touche pas à mes mœurs (Hands Off My Morality), which defends Moroccan values and principles.

Earlier I was saying that we were gaining some freedom of speech. But I think I need to add some nuance to that now. Indeed, social networks do allow us, often anonymously, to share opinions and experiences that would previously have been kept secret. Access to the internet and to mobile phones and increased freedom of the press enable today's Moroccan society to discuss many more topics than when I was growing up, under the reign of King Hassan II and his lapdog media. But for those living lives of transgression, the edict of silence remains all-powerful. And moral issues are causing appalling abuses. Honour killings, beatings and humiliations are the lot of hundreds of single mothers, homosexuals and 'liberated' women. The patent lack of choice in our society, the constant friction between different ways of life and the exploitation of religion all play a role in prompting violent outbursts.

And then, two tragic events occurred to complete the sombre turn of those early days of summer in 2015. On 14 June, two young women named only as Sanae and Sihame, out shopping for food in the souk of Inezgane, a small southern town, were attacked by a stallholder who accused them of wearing their skirts too short and of compromising their modesty. The man was backed by a highly charged mob that went after the women. Fearing for their safety, they took refuge in a shop, to wait for the police to come and knock some sense into these out-of-control bystanders. Picked up by the police, the women were referred to the courts the following day. They were charged under article 483: 'Whoever, by their voluntary state of nudity or by the obscenity of their gestures or actions, commits a public infringement of modesty shall be punished by imprisonment of between one month and two years and by a fine of between 120 and 500 dirhams.' Once again civil society was mobilised online. On Facebook, activist Boutaina Elmakoudi published a video that was watched more than forty thousand times, in which she challenges her fellow citizens. 'It's not just the case of these two girls, it's a generalised shadow over our personal liberty. A Daesh-inspired mentality is infecting our country and risks reaching such a scale that it will curtail our citizens' liberty,' she wrote at the time.

The case prompted an immense wave of solidarity for Sanae and Sihame, and a rash of sit-ins spread around the country under the slogan 'It's no crime to wear a dress'. Some twelve hundred Moroccan lawyers lent their support. Activists and anonymous supporters voiced concern about the possibility of a backward step for women's rights and accused the authorities of conceding too much ground to fundamentalists and conservatives. On 13 July, the Inezgane court acquitted the two women.

Then in Fez on 30 June, in the middle of Ramadan, a man was chased, beaten and eventually almost murdered by a group of furious young men. Dressed in a white djellaba, he several times tried to take refuge inside a car while the group repeatedly called him a 'poof', among other insults. The scene, which took place in the city centre, was filmed and shared on social networks. These unbearably violent images took over our screens just as Islamic State was running its own propaganda campaign across the social platforms. By a horrifying effect of juxtaposition, the Moroccan video gave the impression of taking place in a town under jihadist control. This time, the authorities acted decisively against the aggressors, but the conflict latent in the heart of Moroccan society was clear for all to see. The justice and interior ministers then published a joint statement announcing 'legal proceedings for any individual or group of individuals taking justice and the laws into their own hands, by acting on their own volition to punish other people'. The Fez attackers were landed with four months in prison. But how many times did I hear that the man's behaviour was a provocation and that really he was asking for what they did to him?

In March 2016, in Beni Mellal, two gay men were attacked in their home, and the video showing them bloody, beaten and humiliated later went viral. Worse still: one of the victims was summoned before the judge. Following the video's release at the end of the month, I gave vent to my feelings in the following article for French newspaper *Libération*, titled 'Si j'avais été un homme à Beni Mellal' – 'If I'd been a man in Beni Mellal'.

At the beginning of March, in the heart of Morocco, two homosexual men were violently attacked by a group of men. The pair were arrested by the police, while those responsible for the attack were allowed to go free. One of the victims was condemned to four months' imprisonment. Two of the attackers were given two-month suspended sentences. The second victim is due to appear before the judge on 4 April.

We have all, at times, played the game of wondering 'What would I have done if I were living in Berlin in 1939?', 'How would I have reacted if I'd been in Kigali in 1994?' and the like. Personally, I wonder what I would have done if, instead of being born in a middle-class neighbourhood in Rabat, I'd been born gay in the small town of Beni Mellal; if, one night, while I was with a man, other men had broken in – men after my scalp, baying for blood, ready to tear me to shreds? And while they'd beaten, humiliated, filmed and insulted me, if I'd have considered that I was not only their victim but that also, in the eyes of the law, this made me guilty? And that the police who might come to arrest my tormenters would arrest me too and that, amid laughter, of course, they would take me to prison?

And whether, instead of having parents who taught me that no religion can justify hatred, violence, the murder of prostitutes and expulsion of unbelievers, I had been a killer of poofs, a layer-down of the law, an unassailable misogynist? If, like some of my fellow citizens, I'd been born convinced that lechers, adulterers, gays, unmarried and deflowered women should all be locked up? Whether I'd have hated the West, Jews, lesbians and liberated women? Whether, instead of being born a girl in a family where my body was my own domain, where it was a given that this body was worthy of respect, of love and of pleasure, whether instead of that I'd had to act in secret if I wanted a single kiss, again in secrecy get rid of any child that might begin to grow in me but to whom I could not guarantee an education?

Of course, I will be accused of not loving my country, of not respecting my religion and my identity. I will be told that you don't compromise over immorality, that Morocco is not Sweden and that the condemnation of debauchery, of free love and of relationships between people of the same sex are among our most fundamental principles. Others, from the security of their French university faculty offices, may perhaps accuse me of purveying 'orientalist clichés' and of fuelling Islamophobic discourse. To the latter I would recommend they go and see the adulterous women and the homosexuals, whose punishments are far from fantasies invented by me, where they sit rotting in our prisons.

I know the extent to which all of this depends on 'what if's and flimsy possibilities. That is, of course, in the nature of an arbitrary regime. I have been very lucky and perhaps I should be happy simply to enjoy that. There is a certain presumptuousness in my trying on the shoes of those whose steps are headed to hell. For I've always had my parents, I grew up in my nice neighbourhood, I've always read all the books I wanted to, I have travelled and studied. But I have to say that in Morocco I have met hundreds of people who have not had all this and who, nonetheless, believe that we should live and let live, that every human being has a right to dignity and to safety. This is not just the morality of the middle class or of the West; nothing about it runs contrary to the core principles of Moroccan culture. The path of enlightenment is the privilege of no single people and no one religion; it should lie within reach of us all.

JAMILA

'MEN'S CAUSE'

I have never ever talked about sex with our housekeeper. For me, it is unthinkable to broach the subject with this woman, even though she has been sharing my home for the past twenty years. We, the pair of us, represent two entirely antithetical types of women. At fifty, she has never married and, if we believe the crucial importance of morality and religion in her life, she is a virgin. She lives and works in our house. She provides for a large proportion of her family's needs and they don't hesitate to call on her whenever a problem arises, yet, nonetheless, they pay little attention to her. Because she's a woman and because she has no husband. Pious and practising, she is, I know, upset by my way of life. I smoke, I drink, I go out when I like. I have as many male friends as girlfriends. I imagine that, when I was a teenager, she must have been utterly shocked by the parties we organised, at which girls and boys flaunted their long 'slow dances'.

So I have a fairly clear idea of our housekeeper's views: she is conservative, and she must be judging me without ever saying so. When my first novel came out, I had an opportunity to see her in a completely new light.

One evening, we are alone in the kitchen and she says to me, with a mischievous look: *You know, I know what your book is about.* I smile, a little embarrassed by the conversation she is drawing me into. I am also afraid she will try to pull me up on my morals. *You write about people obsessed with sex, don't you? Because, in Morocco, you know, there are a lot of those. In my neighbourhood, lots of women talk to me about this.*

First revelation: my prudish and moralising housekeeper talks to her neighbours about sex! I am gobsmacked.

I've a friend who lives close to my house. She told me that her husband wants to have sex three or four times a day. He doesn't ask what she wants. You see what I'm saying? she says. Yes, I see: he rapes her. I realise that I don't know how to say 'rape' in Arabic, but my housekeeper and I have understood each other.

Lots of men are like that, she goes on. *The women work, they bring up the children, they look after the house. On top of that, they have to do everything monsieur fancies and they're endlessly falling pregnant. Luckily, some men prefer to see other girls in the neighbourhood so they leave their wives alone.*

Other girls? I ask if she is talking about prostitutes. *Well, yes, of course. There are so many. They're very young. You know, even the Saudis come to us for the prostitutes. In Rabat, they had a huge villa built where they entertain the young girls. They have to strip completely naked and dance for the men. After a while, they throw banknotes on the floor and say: 'Roll in them and if you've sweated enough, you can keep all the notes that stick to you.'*

I don't know if this story is altogether true and I have few means of checking it. Nonetheless, it is true that rich men from the Gulf States come regularly to Morocco to enjoy the unfortunately legendary Moroccan prostitutes. So partial have these clients become that many have even shifted base to Morocco: a wave of immigration that is not to everyone's taste.

It's pure misery for the women, my housekeeper goes on, apparently determined to tell all. *In the neighbourhood, you know, there's that girl who has Aids. She kept it quiet for a long time, but we found out in the end. The guy who gave it to her dropped her like a hot potato and vanished. Now she's got no one at all. It's sad, all these things that go on. In lots of families there are girls who get pregnant by their uncle or even their father. They don't talk about it. Either the families hide them or they kill themselves.* I point out to her that all these situations arise from great hypocrisy and no one daring to report crimes in their anxiety to avoid dishonour. I try to explain that a society in which women had more freedom would not necessarily be contrary to the faith but rather could allow us to protect women better. To my great surprise, she agrees. *All of this*, she says, *is bad for the cause of Islam. There's only one cause that does well out of it: men's cause.*

'There are girls who get pregnant by their uncle or even their father. Either the families hide them or they kill themselves.'

MUSTAPHA

A POLICEMAN IN RABAT

Mustapha is the father of one of my friends. At my friend's suggestion, I come to meet him at their house in a poor district of the capital. He's a genial man who's been doing this job for more than twenty-five years. These days he mostly does deskwork, but he still has a detailed knowledge of the local criminal landscape.

The truth, he tells me, is that we can't apply the laws. Honestly, are we going to arrest all the couples we see holding hands in order to check they're married? We know perfectly well where the young people meet, but we pretend not to see them. Of course, the police sometimes run checks in the hotels, but that's often so that we can protect the girls, for example in the tourist cities, where there's a lot of prostitution. The truth is that everything actually comes down to money. Those who have the means can do what they like. It's unfortunate but when we're asked to bust prostitutes, of course it's the ones who get paid in vegetables who we bring in, not the rest. The prostitutes who go round in luxury cars earn more in one night than I will in my lifetime. Quite frankly, no policeman likes being forced to make arrests over morality issues. We have better things to do. What's really distressing is that people want to mete out justice themselves, in the name of religion; they think they have the right to choose whether other people live or die.

Besides, if I'm completely honest, the situation works out fairly well. In Morocco, sex is a very, very profitable business. It does well for the police, for the caretakers, for the pimps, for everyone. Some men go around boasting about how they're always praying and how their beards come down to here, but that doesn't stop them seeing whores or even picking up boys in side streets. We know all about that! Prostitutes, young lovers and adulterous couples have to pay up now and then. There's no morality in it, no faith: it's the law of cash. The law of what speaks loudest.

It's not always easy for young people. With the internet and all that, they're out of step with their parents. I have three daughters and I talk to them about everything. I don't have no-go subjects. I know it's better to talk, otherwise the girls will take many risks. I always tell them they have to respect the country's culture and values and that, more than anything, they have to be discreet. Never upset people. But I trust them. Much more than my boys, who haven't always been very focused at school and give me lots of trouble. My eldest daughter has her first-class degree and she's already earning her own living. So now I let her go out as much as she likes. She has her driving licence. She goes travelling with her friends. That's no problem for me.

'In Morocco, sex is a very, very profitable business. It does well for the police, for the caretakers, for the pimps, for everyone.'

I know that the way I talk can come across as strange, especially in my line of work. But I take that on board and I've never tried to act tough. Young people don't talk much about love. There's no place for emotions in this country. The only thing that counts is money. When you've got money, you're free. The laws are mostly for the poor. I don't want to give my children the childhood I had, with so much shouting and violence. My sister, who I've always looked after, has found a very good job. She often says that if I'd not been there, she wouldn't have the life she has now. That's a source of pride.

Morocco is not Sweden and we can't just import what they do wholesale. People aren't ready to have sexual freedom like in Europe. But my work as a cop, on the ground, has shown me that there's a lot of hypocrisy and violence behind what goes on here. Here, because of hshouma, we never talk about paedophilia, incest, rape, the prostitution of minors . . . I've seen terrible things in my life. I've picked babies out of dustbins. We have to be able to talk about everything before we can tackle our problems.

'WHO'D WANT A GIRL LIKE ME?'

F is a prostitute. I've no need to ask her to be sure. I've only to watch her, as the men in the room are doing. She is sitting at a hotel bar in Casablanca. She's a pretty girl, wearing too much make-up and looking altogether too polished. Perhaps she's trying to look like one of those Arabic pop stars our Moroccan boys dream about. F is twenty-five and looks much older.

My parents came to Casablanca when they were young, to get out of poverty. They're from the south of Morocco. They are country people and, though they've been living in the city a long time, at heart they haven't moved far. I grew up in a poor neighbourhood, with three sisters and two brothers. My parents are illiterate and they didn't take much interest in our education. I stopped school young, but I like reading and seeing films. I think I could have been a good student with a bit of help. You know, every day you're meant to kiss your parents' foreheads in thanks for being able to study. But I'm ignorant and there's nothing I can do.

We didn't talk about sex or love with my parents. There are things you don't do. They were working long hours, they were always worried, always tired. They brought us up the hard way. They yelled at us all the time. And they used to hit us. My sisters and I helped our mother with the house and looking after our brothers. By twelve I could do everything, I knew how to keep a household.

I hated it where we lived. I used to get hassled by the boys, there were lots of drugs and lots of violence. When you're a girl, you have to fight to make people respect you. I always wanted to come here, to the centre of Casablanca, where the shops and the best restaurants are, where I could have worked in a shop or as a waitress.

In my neighbourhood everyone knew some girls who went with men. Young girls and older ones. I remember one woman whose husband had left her. I think she had two or three children. Everyone knew that that was how she could afford her children's milk. You mustn't think people don't know. Even my mother knows perfectly well what I do.

I started working in a hair salon when I was seventeen. I was already quite mature: I had breasts, I looked older than I was. But I didn't like the work and I wasn't very good at it. It was my boss who found a way for me to do massage instead. And that's how it started. In the beginning I was doing massages at a hotel, and from there I got some regular clients. My mother would like me to marry a foreigner so I can get the papers and go abroad, so she doesn't complain. She's pretending not to know.

I've met some very kind men. There are older ones who give me presents and help me. But otherwise it's hard, very hard. I try not to think about the future because otherwise I just sit and cry. I'd like to get married, have children, but I'll have to get far away from here. It makes me feel sick. I've seen too much of this in my life. The men here treat us like dogs. Even the middle-class ones, they're always coming to us. The boys from good families can't sleep with middle-class girls their age, so they come and let off steam with us. They all want to be like in the porn films. You have to flatter them a lot, tell them they're tigers in bed – that keeps them happy.

A group of us girls go to the nightclubs. We'll sit in a corner, order a bottle of white wine and wait. The owners know us and so do the regulars. In the beginning I wasn't careful and there were situations with fights and thefts. Sometimes I was really frightened. But now we always go to the same places and we're careful.

If I'd listened to my father, I'd be a maid in a house or perhaps a waitress, earning a pittance. Or even worse, I'd already have four kids and a husband who'd beat me. Whatever you do, it's very hard for women in this country. If you haven't got parents with money or an education either, you can't escape. Of course, I fear God and

'The boys from good families all want to be like in the porn films.'

I know very well that what I do is haram, but I don't have a choice. What would my family live on without me? My father died five years ago and my mother doesn't work. It's me who gives money to my brothers and sisters. My younger brother has a full beard and wears the jubba, but he never judges me. He's very good to me.

I've been pregnant twice. I aborted them through a girlfriend who knew a doctor. It was hard. I got sick and I couldn't work for weeks and weeks. Luckily, my friend and I live together in the same apartment. She goes out with a pilot who rents the apartment and comes to see her regularly. He's a Muslim. He's very nice and very in love with her. In the streets round about, of course they know what we do, but how could they not? They know life isn't easy for anyone. This is poverty, that's all.

Things have got very difficult in Casablanca. There's a lot of competition. The African women also do prostitution and they'll work for next to nothing. I've heard they also pass on diseases, and that's really frightening.

Moroccan men have the devil between their legs. They always say it's women's fault, but the problem is with them. I would like to go to Europe, have a job, be a mother too. Here there's no one who can help me to get out. Who'd want a girl like me?

MALIKA[*]

MAKING LOVE: THE ORIGINAL SIN

Malika is forty. She's single and has never been married. A doctor, she has been posted to a rural practice, in a deeply conservative region, far from the big urban centres. She lives alone, a long way from her family. Her parents are laid-back. Her religious education was not particularly strict.

We had quite a classic education: it was all about good and evil and respect for your elders. We were never separated from the boys, we threw parties at home, we all travelled together. It was very free. Of course, we never went to nightclubs and, generally speaking, our outings were among a very limited circle of people. But I never found that particularly frustrating.

Like most of the women I have spoken to, Malika cannot recall ever receiving any sex education. *There were no taboos, we didn't live in shame. That said, we never talked about contraception or protection. In any case, if you lose your virginity, you must be married, so problem solved!*

Malika came late to sex. She only met her first boyfriend towards the end of her first year at uni, and her relationship with him was a chaste one. She was twenty-four when, for the first time, one of her friends announced she had slept with a boy one night, just like that.

* This name has been changed.

I was terribly shocked. I started to lecture her, to tell her that now she absolutely had to marry him. Afterwards, I kept thinking about it for days and days. I went back to see her and apologised. That moment stayed with me. I realised that, like everyone else, I'd been conditioned. No one had ever specifically talked to me about virginity, I hadn't given it a thought – and yet I had this very hard-line attitude.

Malika lost her virginity quite late, with a foreigner, an older man, whom she never considered marrying. *By that age, I had left those constraints behind somewhat. While all around me my friends and sisters were marrying as virgins, I concentrated on my studies and won greater personal freedom and financial independence.*

As a doctor, Malika has witnessed extremely difficult situations, scenes she is unlikely to have experienced had she gone on living in her middle-class family cocoon. *Before I became a doctor, I had no idea how common virginity certificates are. That really shocked me. One morning at 8 a.m., back when I was doing my internship in gynaecology, a girl was brought in straight after her wedding night, for me to determine whether she'd been freshly or previously deflowered. I said, categorically, that it was fresh. I'd have covered up for her anyway. That incident left a bitter taste.*

Another time, I fell out with a colleague who wanted to report a single woman in whom we had diagnosed an ectopic pregnancy. She'd begged us to keep her secret. But my colleague was furious. For him, it was more important to betray her to her family than to care for her.

In many ways, Malika's life stands out as different in Moroccan society. Unmarried at forty, she earns a good living in a well-regarded profession. She owns her own apartment and travels a lot, by herself. *Men feel squeezed out by what I stand for, which is the opposite of the submissive and maternal image of the classic Moroccan woman. For men, there's a gap between being liberated about the act of sex and liberation of the mind. Most of them are only liberated for as long as the sex lasts. In their heads, they're already passing judgement.*

So it's no accident that Malika has remained single. She seems to have had many disappointments with men. *My ex went to school in France and he's very liberal, very cool. Yet even he can only imagine marrying a younger woman who's a virgin. And at the same time, he boasts of going to see prostitutes on a regular basis. When I expressed shock at all this, he said: 'You're intolerant. This is my right. I'm allowed both to want to fuck and to marry a virgin.' He didn't consider this in the least contradictory. Like lots of men, his approach to sex is thoroughly immature.* As Malika repeatedly emphasises, men still get to choose, even if they too suffer from the hypocrisy. *At least they have the menu and they can choose 'à la carte'. On the left-hand side, the women they can sleep with. And on the right, the ones they'll marry.*

When I ask her if Morocco's deeply conservative laws concerning sex cause her hardship, Malika stops me straight away. *Not being able to make love to my guy isn't hardship, it drives me round the bend! So we have to be smart. We go to hotels owned by French people who won't ask for our ID. The problem is that I feel completely out of sync. The way people talk is scary, and the more this goes on, the scarier it gets. Hypocrisy is growing here, and conservatism too.*

Malika also struggles with another problem that all the single women I spoke to have mentioned, even some of the widows I was able to meet. In Morocco, it's very hard for an unmarried woman to have a social life. Beyond a certain age, socialising comes to seem impossible for those not in couples. *I've often felt I was rejected because I represent a risk. The other women are scared I'm going to steal their husbands and the husbands are worried that my position as a liberated woman will have a bad influence on their wives. I've lost friends because of this – and I'd never have imagined that. It makes me feel abnormal, like an intruder.*

Once I had a fling with a man. A one-night stand, and I knew that was all it would be. It was the first time I'd done that and I really enjoyed making love without any second thoughts. I told my sister about it, in a light-hearted way. She was absolutely horrified. I didn't understand, I was upset. She's married, she has children and, like many people, now she's safely on the right path, she judges anyone who doesn't fit in. I know single women my age who claim they're still virgins. I don't understand. One of my friends met a man with whom she fell deeply, deeply in love. That girl is no virgin – I know it. Yet when the man suggested they go on holiday together, she refused, claiming she's 'not that kind of girl'. Lots of women do this when they're hoping to marry someone. They play the fearful virgin. They lie down on their backs and pretend to be nervous. Well, I find that degrading.

So Malika lives in relative isolation. Due to fear of criticism, and to weariness too, she has given up sharing her personal life with those closest to her. Her love life is completely off-limits. *My parents pretend they don't know about my boyfriends. One time, I started to talk about someone I liked, but as soon as something actually happened between us, I didn't mention him again. I'd crossed their red line. I'm wary of the power people could have over me. I've fought too hard for this freedom; it would be stupid to give it up now.*

Last year, I got pregnant. I really couldn't have kept it. My mother was ill, my work was taking up a lot of my time and I had no wish to get together with the father. It was obvious to me that I should have an abortion. The girl who's been my cleaner for years comes from the countryside and she was amazing once she understood my situation. She said: 'Don't worry. I'll bring it up for you, I'll look after it. Who cares about the father? We don't even need one. As they say, if no one is feeding you, no one has any rights over you.' In contrast, my enlightened, well-educated cousin shrieked: 'Oh my God, how dreadful! You'll have to go abroad and hide for months.' She stopped calling and I could tell she was ashamed of me. I didn't consider it at all shameful. I couldn't have brought up a child at that point in my life; if I was going to have a

*termination, it was not out of shame at becoming pregnant
outside marriage, but rather for practical reasons.*

*So I had a termination. There were four of us in the wait-
ing room: me, able to afford a child but not currently ready; a
married woman who already had lots of children and couldn't
cope with another; a prostitute who seemed quite relaxed and
was talking loudly on her phone: 'But why did they give her a
general anaesthetic? They only gave me a local last time!'; and
there was a woman whose face haunted me for days afterwards. She was wearing a djellaba and headscarf, and her
appearance suggested great poverty. She was trying to bargain
with the nurse, explaining that she didn't have the means to
pay and that she'd come back the following
week. The nurse explained to her: 'Each
week you wait, it will cost more.' I should
have paid for her. What would become of
her? With luck, she might turn to prostitution to pay for her abortion. Worse, she*

**'With luck, she
might turn to
prostitution to pay
for her abortion.'**

*might have committed suicide. That happens more often than
we realise. I often think of us four women and reflect that
the new draft bill would have helped none of us, and yet we
represent the majority of abortion cases in Morocco today. At
the time, I wanted to shout it from the rooftops, to tell the
world. I couldn't stand the fact that I was forced to hide it, to
experience it as shameful when of course I'd taken no pleasure
in this decision.*

*Thanks to my profession and income, I was able to resolve
that situation. But this isn't the case for all single women,*

many of whose lives are tipped into tragedy. One of my friends has just adopted a little girl whose mother is a peasant from the Middle Atlas mountains. The mother gave her daughter to my friend, then went back to her village.

One day, a colleague and I were chatting about that teen mother who set fire to herself during a royal visit. My colleague said, 'You can't call her a victim. She should have faced up to her responsibilities.' I was outraged: what kind of crime deserves such a punishment? She had sex – that was her first crime!

I am sure we still have a very long way to go, and that can feel desperate.

*

In my parents' time, the leaden silence that surrounded sex was not nearly as problematic as it has become today. Only fifty years ago, the great majority of Moroccan women were married while still teenagers; they hardly had a chance to imagine or experience any kind of sex life before marriage. This still applies to many Moroccan women but, in the towns and among the middle class, more and more of them are attending university, working and paying their own way. Between 1987 and 2007, the fertility rate dropped from 4.3 children per woman to 2.33.* Over the same period, the average age of a woman at first marriage increased from twenty-three to twenty-eight years old. Today, 25% of households

---

* These statistics come from Morocco's Higher Planning Commission, an independent governmental statistics institution.

are sustained by a woman alone. In 2012, 51% of graduates were women, and seven out of ten of the best baccalaureate grades were awarded to girls. Society has changed drastically and women's place is vastly different, and yet their rights have not been reviewed in line with these changes.

Women's emancipation is one factor but financial difficulties also explain the boom in unmarried young people. In hard times, it's not exactly easy to insist on sexual abstinence. Yet while their upbringing keeps the focus on virginity, girls are escaping their families' control as soon as they leave home. As everywhere else in the world, they dream about love and, in ever greater numbers, are daring to break taboos, even though they know that most men demand virginity before marriage. In any case, the model of marriage as it used to be practised thirty years ago is no longer our gold standard. Couples want to get to know each other these days, to grow to love each other. But this sexual freedom also leads to feelings of insecurity, guilt and anxiety for unmarried couples.

This whole situation naturally worsens the already very tense relations between Moroccan men and women. Frustration leads to abuse, especially in public places, where women are often harassed. Of course they have the right to work and the duty to pay tax, but they haven't yet altogether won the privilege of walking the streets in peace, sitting on a cafe terrace to smoke a cigarette, etc.

Although better known for his ultra-conservative opinions, in February 2016, MP Abouzaid El Mokri posted a video in which he expressed his admiration for the fairer sex, who, he pointed out, do better academically, contribute more to managing households and uphold the rules of public life, in contrast to our boys, who are treated like kings and are much less driven to succeed. This must be our first revolution: women are taking up more and more space in the public realm. They are reaching high places and they're acting with greater freedom. For the men this is a massive reversal that leaves them on the back foot and that, naturally, leads them to feel profoundly unmoored.

ASMA LAMRABET

'ALL THE RELIGIONS ARE THE SAME WHEN IT COMES TO SEX'

Every time I talk about the possibility of a 'sexual revolution' in Morocco, my interlocutors douse my enthusiasm. For many, the dominance of religion in our society makes legislative change impossible in the near future. So I wonder if it's possible to imagine being a Muslim and having a free and fulfilling sex life without having to account for oneself to either state or society.

Everything indicates that Islamic faith can accept only one kind of sex: conjugal sex, which is therefore heterosexual sex. Muslim societies are shaped around the taboos of fornication, homosexuality, single motherhood, abortion and prostitution. The system persists thanks to a culture of silence, practically an *omertà*, that is preached by the faithful, guaranteed by the laws and enforced by social convention.

Nonetheless, as respected researchers have shown, in Islam's early years sex was far from taboo. In *L'Érotisme arabe* (*Arab Eroticism*), Malek Chebel shows that sex even used to be considered a source of balance and fulfilment for human beings. The purpose of the sexual act is not solely procreation but also pleasure: orgasm is a prelude to the delights promised in paradise. Initially, Islam encouraged sexuality because the religion taught that there was no

reason to render impure anything created by God. This is
Fatima Mernissi's explanation in her book *L'Amour dans
les pays musulmans* (*Love in Muslim Countries*): 'Although
Jesus had no sex life, that of the Prophet Mohammed was a
rich one. And it is described in great detail to the believer
who seeks a guide or model. Both religions advise wari-
ness around desire, but not in the same ways. Christianity
presents sex as a source of downfall . . . More sophisticat-
edly, Islam identifies desire as an enemy that must be isolated and understood, the better to control it.' What's more,
Islamic cultures have long been well known for their sensuality and eroticism. As Mernissi again reminds us, wasn't it
Christians who found Mohammed's display of his conjugal
and sexual contentment unseemly?

Muslims can turn to a long written tradition, led by scholars, that saw no incompatibility between the needs of the
body and the demands of the faith. From the ninth to the
thirteenth centuries, when Islamic civilisation reached its
apogee, literature and the erotic arts flourished. 'The teenagers still all read *The Perfumed Garden* by Sheikh Nefzaoui,
which was written in the fourteenth century because a
prince wanted to know how to make love and achieve the
greatest degree of pleasure. And this text opens with *bismil-
lah*, which means "In the name of God, the most merciful",
novelist Tahar Ben Jelloun reminds me.

From the nineteenth century onwards, the intellectual,
political and economic decline of the Arab world seems
to have proceeded in tandem with increasingly puritanical

views about sex. With the advent of the twentieth century, colonisation was in any case set to impose very restrictive laws in this domain. The aim was to establish a barrier between immigrants from the West and native women, and so to contain the 'unbridled' sensuality of the local population. Moreover, we should remember that the Moroccan penal code's article 489, which bans homosexual sex, is identical to the French penal code's former article 331, which was repealed in 1982. The Moroccan legislation is drawn not from sharia or any other religious source but from substantive laws inherited directly from the French protectorate. In the same period, nascent Islamism decided that the defeat of the Arab world, which had fallen into European control, should in part be blamed on the sexual licence that had prevailed here. In 1929, Hassan Al-Banna, founder of the Muslim Brotherhood, wrote of Egypt: 'Why has the country fallen into subjugation? Is it because we strayed from the sharia?' Women's freedom, homosexuality and free love were singled out as reprehensible idealisms, and the legal interpretations around sex became ever narrower and more intransigent.

For Abdelwahab Bouhdiba, Tunisian author of *Sexuality in Islam*, the great 1975 classic text, this restrictive, puritanical, gloomy view of sex runs contrary to the very spirit of Islam. For him, 'To rediscover the meaning of sexuality is to rediscover the meaning of God, and conversely.' And: 'Sexuality properly performed is tantamount to freedom assumed.' In his book, Bouhdiba recalls a long-obscured Islamic perspective on sex: that of a joyous, fulfilling relationship with fleshly pleasure. He describes a culture in which the body is not denied or constrained and in which coitus resembles a moment of prayer. But in his view, the solution cannot be achieved by a wholesale copying of the western model on to Muslim societies. A third way must be found and sexual freedom achieved through faith, not against it.

Contrary to what we might think, Moroccan clerics are by no means silent on subjects relating to sex. Quite the opposite: sex is without question one of the commonest topics addressed by the most popular preachers, who sometimes come up with rather baroque scenarios. Among the most controversial of these fatwas are those of the late Sheikh Zamzami, an influential preacher from Tangier. He made headlines by asserting that Islam would permit sexual congress with a corpse, on condition that the corpse be that of the person's spouse. In an interview for an Arabic weekly, Imam Zamzami also claimed that, from the religious point of view, recourse to sex toys is perfectly permissible. Muslim women have the right to use carrots, bottles and other objects to assuage their sexual desires . . . 'Permitting masturbation is intended to help young women and men not to slip into sin. We live in times when everything is pushing young people towards sexual experiences outside marriage. Masturbation is, therefore, a temporary solution for young Muslims, until they're able to marry. So allowing masturbation has a religious purpose: to keep our youth from temptation to mortal sin.'

On the Arabic satellite networks, the *ulama* (experts on Islamic law) never stop talking about sex. On Al Jazeera, Sheikh Al-Qaradawi, without doubt the most famous Sunni preacher, presents a programme called *Sharia and Life*, which is watched by tens of thousands. Very often, the topic is sexual issues: advising men how to assuage their 'uncontrollable desires', advising the use of masturbation, etc. In 2008, a Dutch imam forbade female Muslims in the Netherlands from riding bicycles, for 'straddling the bicycle saddle induces sexual excitation in women and so, from this point of view, the bicycle becomes a forbidden object'. In 2007, two professors from Al-Azhar University in Egypt suggested 'that a woman may breastfeed her colleague up to five times in order to establish a breast-based relationship with him', such that the two people may remain alone in an office together, their relationship being that of a mother with her nursing child. Also under the heading 'Sex', a recent fatwa banned women from touching bananas and cucumbers, because they look like the male sex organ.

In 2007, two professors suggested 'that a woman may breastfeed her colleague up to five times in order to establish a breast-based relationship with him', such that the two people may remain alone in an office together, their relationship being that of a mother with her nursing child.

In order to shed some light on this issue, I went to meet Asma Lamrabet, a doctor, theology researcher and key figure among Morocco's reformist thinkers. I found her in Rabat, at the Centre for Women's Studies in Islam, based at the Rabita Mohammadia of Ulama, a highly prestigious and respected religious institution.

I began to work on the texts in order to answer a question that's ultimately very personal: how should I, as a Muslim woman, go about achieving spiritual fulfilment? Why, at every step, must I answer for myself with reference to my faith?

Women live with a sword of Damocles hanging over their heads. Anyone can say whatever they like in the name of the faith. Any time someone wants to justify their dominance over you, they toss you the line 'The Koran says so.' We need to give women the tools to argue their corner against this widespread religious ignorance. We mustn't accept anything and everything just because it's said to be sacred. This is why I feel I must go back to the sources, to find out what they actually say.

We are living in societies in which religious influence has strengthened and in which women are charged with representing Muslim identity. The woman's body bears a terrible burden. The visibility of the women in any given society indicates the degree of its Islamisation. Honour, image, cultural education, virtue: all these weigh down on our women's shoulders.

I don't work on questions of sexuality. I should admit that I actually avoid them because they do rather trouble me. These questions are very difficult to disentangle and to analyse in the current psychological climate. I hope that this will come gradually. Our society is so split, so Manichaean, that we have to go back and begin at the beginning, which means asking: how should we approach religion?

I was chatting with some American researchers earlier. One of them had given her Moroccan students a dissertation to write with the title: 'What does religion mean to you in one or two words?' And the great majority of her female students had replied with the word 'fear'. This is awful! We've created this image of a vengeful God, a punitive religion. From classes at the public nurseries right through to the Koranic madrasas, everywhere, we say 'Fear God', otherwise you're not a good Muslim. In this context, it is clear that we're also afraid of sex. We need a complete overhaul of the way we educate girls and boys, to teach religion to them as an ethics of liberation, of emancipation, instead of as this severe black-and-white morality. We need to re-examine our cultural foundations.

The Koran is notably silent on questions of sex. For example, I have found absolutely nothing about virginity, even in the Prophet's statements. He personally led a relatively untrammelled sex life. This obsession with virginity, which sits at the heart of our societies, is primarily a peculiarly Mediterranean characteristic. Interpretations have followed, offered by ulama who claim that the faith itself requires virginity before marriage. But not one person has yet been able to show me a clear text on this. There are nothing but generalities in the texts.

One thing is clear: the Koran is primarily addressed to the insan (the human being), which has no gender. We are first and foremost human beings. This realisation naturally raised questions for me as a woman, because I feel we have always been classed as inferior compared to the norm, which is the male. Now, when one is considered a human being and not an inferior being, that changes an awful lot of things when it comes to sex! 'Gendered' sex, as we have been obliged to consider it, does not exist. Besides, let's not forget that first Judaism – which is very harsh on questions of sex – and then Catholicism have had an extensive influence on interpretations of the Koranic text. The first exegetes did not work in isolation; they were already immersed in monotheistic cultures and in their world views. And I would add one more crucial thing: misogyny is common to all humankind. It is not specific to Islam – far from it. I'm surprised that we still get this kind of anthropological reading. For me, all the religions are the same when it comes to sex.

The difference is that the Koran is silent on many topics and offers margins for interpretation that allow us to exercise a degree of common sense. But this silence can also be turned to bad ends by exegetes. On sex within marriage, for example, there is actually scope for eroticisation and for sexual freedoms that would not be acceptable in other religions. Let's take the famous and controversial verse that's so often trotted out by those who wish to prove either that Islam is misogynist or that Muslim men should have total control over their wives' bodies: 'Your wives are as fields ("harth") for you. You may enter your fields from any place you want' (Koran 2:223). This is one of the most commonly found translations and it is in fact a very literal one. So I went on to research the conditions around the revelation of this text. At that time, the men of Medina who had married women from Mecca had complained that their wives were refusing to have sex 'from behind'. The women believed in an old superstition, doubtless carried over from the Hebraic tradition, according to which this risked making their children blind.

In fact, this verse is intended to 'liberate' local morality, to convince believers of their partners' freedoms in sexual activity. Broadly it says: 'Carry out this act in any way you please.' There is one lone exegete – a Shiite, as it happens; they're often the more liberal – in whose commentary I found a different and thrilling translation. Rather than translate *harth* as 'fields of labour' or similar, he translated it as 'a source of life'. And that changes everything! We are teaching our women that they must allow anything to be done to them, that they may even be raped, that they must accept everything their husband does. But from this new perspective, the woman becomes a source of wealth and sensuality – not a passive object.

We have to acknowledge it: we are a frustrated people. Aren't the Gulf countries the biggest consumers of porn in the world? We are fed a zealot's diet of Islamic discourse that is restricted to what's halal and what's haram, and which, while claiming to cover women up, manages effectively to hyper-sexualise them. For me, to lean more towards spirituality is also to desexualise one's body. I wanted to free myself from the idea that being a woman is my primary identity.

Feminists are afraid of tackling causes related to sexual rights. I have an anecdote about this. Two years ago, I gave a *lecture where the audience was made up of older* ulama, *all very attached to tradition and the orthodoxy. I had prepared a paper on women in Islam and I had somewhat adapted it for my audience, without, of course, compromising my central point. I was working with a very classic text – and yet I was attacked. It was as if I were facing the judges of the Inquisition. They told me: 'You're westernised. You want Muslim women to be like western women!', 'You want to legalise homosexuality in Morocco.' I was only arguing for one thing: equality between men and women. Yet even that was inconceivable to them.*

I'm employed by a religious institution, I work on the sacred texts and I owe it to myself to do this with the greatest delicacy. For me, the main thing is to liberate women and from there to allow women to make their own choices. For when we talk about sexual freedom, we're also talking about models. What kind of model do we want for our society? The only model that's been theorised so far is a 'western' one (though I can't stand that crude term), which promotes moral freedom and would cause real upset here. Personally, I prefer to follow a decolonialist line of thinking. I don't trust hegemonies or any models we might simply copy wholesale. I feel we need to be building something, inventing something brand-new.

Like a Jewish feminist struggling with an obsolete Hebraic law, I am fighting against a particular interpretation of the Koran that, in our patriarchal societal structure, leads to women's oppression. For, unlike what we so often hear, Islam's spiritual message is one of emancipation. Take abortion:

according to the prophetic traditions, there is a period of clemency that allows a woman to abort at any time up to the end of the second month of pregnancy. In the same way, the prohibition of co-education is nothing but a selective and macho reading of the Koran: historically, mosques, our sites of knowledge and debate, were sometimes mixed. Women were not excluded from what was sacred. Our forebears succeeded in coupling their faith with their fleshly needs. We need to create a new and positive model of sexuality that works for our own era. In the past, sex was not put on display but it wasn't quite so hidden either. We have lost sight of what's natural, lost our freedom to speak up, in the interests of a puritanism that is foreign to our culture.

I am tired of hearing women being compared to jewellery: woman as a gemstone or a sweet that must be covered up to protect it from greedy eyes. Even if we lock her away, imprison her, it's always for her own good, always for her protection. Woman is fitna – *temptation; woman is* awra – *prohibited to the gaze. We rant about how she must retreat to the hearth and we go into excessive detail about how she dresses and about her body. But the Koran never talks about women in this way. For Islam, women are first and foremost free human beings, endowed with good sense, intelligence and logic.*

I'm sorry too that intimacy, compassion and affection, all concepts that are very present in Islam historically, should be set aside to make way for cold and heartless rigidity. And I wonder what place remains for love in our society. My generation overrated love: we were sentimental and proud of it.

I find young people today are much more pragmatic. They claim to be acting rationally, not to be led solely by their feelings.

Wahhabism is a cultureless ideology. In Morocco we are lucky to have cultural Islam and we absolutely must protect this culture, which favours inclusivity. We do have macho tendencies, but we're not a hopeless case. Actually, when you show our young people an Islam that is open and liberating, many find it a great comfort.

I'm optimistic because I feel that we have nonetheless made some progress. Ten years ago, we wouldn't have dared mention some of the things we're discussing now. Even though some of the reactions have been utterly barbaric, at least they can now be freely discussed. Unfortunately, our faith is taught as a clutch of rigid dogmas, centred around the polarity of halal–haram, without encouraging the believer to exercise their own critical appreciation, to develop their own sense of ethics. This liberation will change many things and the prospect does frighten some people. If we can present piety as a means of liberation, you will see tongues begin to untie, bodies be liberated and minds emancipated alongside. We cannot liberate the body alone and leave the soul behind. Even when it comes to elections, think how differently a 'liberated' citizen might act.

A QUESTION OF IDENTITY

THE LESSON OF THE WEST

However challenging this will be for those whose weapon of choice is caricature, the people I have met and who have talked to me are no 'secular elite'. They are women from all walks of life, each of whom has her own story, her own aspirations. None of them seemed to be attacking some idea of 'Moroccan identity'; their only aim was to live freely and to do with their bodies as they wished.

In her essay *We Should All Be Feminists*, Nigerian novelist Chimamanda Ngozi Adichie describes how a Nigerian academic once explained to her that feminism is 'un-African', saying bluntly that it's 'not our culture'. For Islamists too, a universal feminism is nothing but a Trojan horse from the West. For them, Enlightenment principles are a delusion. Have they not served to legitimise colonisation? Aren't they pure fakery, since western leaders forget all about them at the first sight of a juicy oil deal? Once, when I was defending the idea of decriminalising sexual relations in Morocco to a roomful of listeners, a man stood up, clearly furious, and quite simply accused me of wanting to spread homosexuality and to turn Morocco into a vast whorehouse. And if you feel inclined to say yes, actually you do envy the West's sexual freedom, the equality of the sexes there, western women's freedom to walk outside at night in peace, you are considered a traitor. Then doubtless you will be parried with that old and so-seductive argument: 'A woman who flaunts herself in a bikini, who submits to the tyranny of the erotic, is she freer than a woman in hijab? Are western women really happier?'

When I tell French friends, again, how West-obsessed the far side of the Mediterranean can be, they are doubtful, even irritated. 'Oh, stop going on about the West. Colonisation ended ages ago. We can't blame ourselves for everything.' True, the colonial powers are no more and relations with former colonies have relaxed. But since the 1990s, successive wars in the Arab world have been experienced as humiliations, and the hegemony of the western way of life is seen as a kind of colonisation by stealth. For Abdelhak Serhane, author of *L'amour circoncis* (*Circumcised Love*), 'all western culture has achieved is to bulldoze the modes of traditional identification and to leave the individual surrounded by troubling ambiguities and sources of conflict'. The feeling of being pushed into modernity and globalisation reinforces people's determination to keep alive the patriarchy, a symbol of the identity that's under threat. The realm of sex becomes the only space where men can exercise their dominance.

For Salafi Muslims, the West is precisely what not to wish for: a demonstration of transparency to excess, where anything can be said and everything can be seen, where people are fucking everywhere and all the time, and where women's bodies no longer occasion any modesty at all. To give in to this would be to risk a plunge into chaos. To accept women's freedom would be to accelerate the breakdown of the social order and to condemn an entire culture and all its traditions. Besides, talk to an Islamist about the West and you will see how soon he brings the conversation around to women, homosexuality or sexual freedom. For these people, the principal features of the West are 'moral anarchy' and 'sexual deviance'. A study (*Islam & the West*) run between 1995 and 2001 by an American team, Ronald Inglehart and Pippa Norris, showed that the greatest differences of opinion between the Muslim world and the West were not over democratic values or political systems but over the role of women and questions relating to sex. For them, 'the cultural gulf separating Islam from the West involves Eros far more than Demos.'

The feeling of being pushed into modernity and globalisation reinforces people's determination to keep alive the patriarchy, a symbol of the identity that's under threat.

All too often, the debate is reduced to each side pointing their finger at and caricaturing the other. Conservatives talk with great contempt of what they call the 'secular tendencies', by which they mean modernists who call for progress – in conservatives' mouths that last word should be spat to the floor. For them, I am obviously part of this westernised elite, enjoying privileges and disconnected from the realities of most of my fellow citizens. But does that make my voice entirely irrelevant? And even so, must I, like a large tranche of Morocco's middle class, make do with a life of secrecy? Should I enjoy in my private sphere freedoms that are in fact prohibited by law? And – because I can afford it – should I behave as I wish in the public spaces reserved for people of my own social class? For a long time, I thought so. For a long time, I bowed to the notion that to impose my views on others amounted to a kind of condescension. Now I think the only thing that matters is the validity of my argument. My position is grounded in universal values and I utterly reject the idea that identity, religion or any historic heritage should dispossess individuals of rights that are universal and inalienable.

In fact, by setting up a Muslim identity founded on virtue and abstinence in contrast to a western culture of depravity, we entirely deny our own cultural heritage. The issue is neither identity nor morality but rather a question of politics. We may suppose that if Muslims don't have sexual rights, this is because most of the regimes they live under rely on the rejection of individual liberties. Ordinary devout citizens are not permitted to think for themselves or to take decisions in good conscience. Similarly, they may not make love with whomever they like. As the British-Egyptian sociologist Shereen El Feki wrote in the *Revue des Deux Mondes* in June 2015, 'religion is a tool of social control, particularly over women and young people. The greater the pressure upon a regime, the more heavily it will repress sexuality under the veil of Islam.'*

'In the 1970s,' sociologist Abdessamad Dialmy explained to me, 'following the sexual revolution in Europe and the United States, some Arab intellectuals became interested in questions around sex and the body.' Witness the books of Abdelwahab Bouhdiba, Fatima Mernissi, Assia Djebar and Malek Chebel, among others. Now, over the last ten years or so, a new generation of intellectuals, mostly from Lebanon and Egypt, are more directly confronting questions of sexual freedom in Muslim countries.

Nonetheless, on the ground, activism remains focused on problems to do with equality of the sexes. Greater emphasis on rights, the struggle for access to education, health, employment and contraception: feminists have achieved a huge amount in fifty years. The struggle against sexual oppression is one battle that remains to be fought.

---

* 'Chair et Charia', *Revue des Deux Mondes*, June 2015

MAHA SANO

PUSSY-NAMING

Maha Sano is a freethinking, creative and startling young woman. We meet in early 2015 in a cafe in central Rabat, close to the apartment where she lives by herself. She tells me about the day in Paris that she saw a performance of Eve Ensler's infamous play *The Vagina Monologues*. Thrilled by the piece, in 2012 she decided to produce the play in Morocco. She worked with the charity Théâtre Aquarium to bring together women from all social classes and backgrounds and to set up a discussion space for them. The aim was to find out what these women called their vaginas. Located in El Akkari, a working-class area of Rabat, Théâtre Aquarium strives to enable women and other marginalised groups to use drama as a means of self-expression. Its principal mission is 'the establishment of equality between the sexes and the dissemination of gender cultures by means of art'.

Sano describes how she worked: *We listened to dozens of women, and the ways they talked about sex were mostly very sad. It seems they felt it was more appropriate to express themselves as victims. Had they enjoyed their experiences or claimed to do so, they evidently feared being likened to prostitutes. In general, we tend to confine women to the role of victim. Look at the debate over abortion: we felt that this right should be reserved for women who are victims. In any case, that is what the proposed legislation offers: those who have had consensual sex have no right to a termination. We entirely deny any right to pleasure, and it's arguably in this way that the state maintains its control over the female body.*

At the same time, the discussion groups were very joyous and we laughed a lot. I remember one of the women said this incredible thing: 'If the hymen didn't exist, that would be freedom.' You should know that this kind of female gathering is not exceptional. In poor neighbourhoods, women come together in the afternoons and talk about their families, their children and . . . sex. Sometimes they invite singers whose songs tell very explicit, sexual stories. These meetings provide a breathing space, time out in a country where sex education is very repressive. When we talk to women about their genitals, we tell them to hide 'their problem', to keep their legs together. We always talk about menstruation in very violent terms. The menses are associated with something impure and dirty, with a kind of original curse.

> **'When the actors said the equivalent of the word "pussy", the audience would burst into laughter; they were embarrassed and liberated at the same time.'**

We ended up putting on the play and, during the months of the performances (June and November 2012), I really sensed the theatre was at boiling point. When the actors said the equivalent of the word 'pussy', the audience would burst into laughter; they were embarrassed and liberated at the same time. In Arabic, the word 'vagina' is extremely rude; that is, it's mostly used as an insult. People told me that hearing it aloud was genuinely refreshing. One gentleman who had come with his daughters admitted his eyes were opened by the show.

Our play follows the story of a typical Moroccan woman from childhood into adulthood. It shows the extent to which female sexuality is blocked and denied, both within the home and in our education system. If a woman talks about her vagina or her own sexuality, she is highly likely to be answered with a slap. In any case, the vocabulary available to her is so very violent that it encourages us to keep this talk taboo and not try to articulate it.

Some conservative Arabic media criticised the play harshly. The newspaper Attajdid, which has close ties with the PJD, accused our cast of using 'provocation and permissiveness as weapons to attack Islamist movements'. I was impressed by the actors, for whom creating these characters was a genuine challenge. Of course the play caused some controversy. Everyone has sex, everyone talks about it, but as soon as you make it the subject of a work of art and so take it 'public', people oppose it in the name of some supposed decency.

During the play, one of the actors says: 'My vagina comes everywhere with me: into my bedroom, to the hammam, to the market, everywhere, even to the mosque'; also 'I keep my legs squeezed tight, squeezed tight because no one must see it. No one should know it's hidden there, between my legs'; and also 'Listening to them, you'd think our vaginas are our misfortune. That we should lock them up. I have to close mine and not open it again until my marriage day.'

During the Arab Spring, we really did gain greater free-dom of speech. The 20 February Movement, which arose in the wake of these revolutions of youth and democracy, made a great difference. Our show was on during that same period, and that helped a lot. It was a time when people – especially the young people – were really keen to bring the truth to light and put a stop to the rule of hypocrisy.

I don't demand this or that model of society. All I want is to have the choice. You know, after spending so much of your life in this delicate balancing act, you can end up quite paranoid. You can't tell for sure which way's right and which is wrong; sometimes you find you're even afraid of your own thoughts and reactions. For me, working on The Vagina Monologues *was more than anything a way of prompting women to recon-sider, a way of breaking them out of the conventions we've built around them. We get used to the way our bodies are viewed by society and to the words used about them. Taking back control of our bodies also demands reworking our lan-guage and our vocabulary, which hold a mirror to our macho culture. I should add: our version of the play is titled* Dialy, *which means 'mine', or rather: 'It's mine!'*

ABDESSAMAD DIALMY

'QUIET, WE'RE FUCKING'

I met Professor Dialmy in Rabat in June 2015. He's a sociologist who has made sex the main subject of his research. He is considered a pioneer in his field.

Sex is an extremely tense topic in Morocco. It's often possible to discern three stages in the approach a society takes to legislation for sexual practices. At the first stage, we see that official norms and prevailing sexual practices are broadly in step. Practices remain substantially regulated by norms, which come from religion. Broadly speaking, sex tends to be solely conjugal. In Morocco, we are at the second stage, when norms continue to be religious and conservative, while practices are breaking away and secularising – albeit without explicit admission that this is the case. Our practices have pushed ahead of our norms. Morocco is in a transitional phase. We may indeed call it hypocrisy, for Moroccans know that the disjunct is real.

As for the Islamists, they have a social theory. In their view, sexual practices in Morocco today are deviant and Moroccans must be set back on the straight and narrow. They believe we are living in a kind of sexual lawlessness, that we've lost our moral bearings and values. Adl Wal Ihsane (the Islamist group Justice and Spirituality) talks of a return to jahiliyya, to the pre-Islamic times of absolute darkness, ignorance and depravity. For Islamists, Islam has no need to reform its conceptual and moral approach to sex. The law is correct; it's the Muslims who are imperfect and must better themselves.

Of course, this 'sexual transition' is more marked in the cities, among the higher social strata, and, in a way, we can say that the women are doing better out of it. Their sexual practices are more advanced than the men's. On the other hand, the men have never been oppressed – until 1926, young single Muslim men even had the right to possess sexual slaves! If a man has sex before marriage, that's bad but he's allowed. But if a young girl does it, she is irreversibly condemned.

One of the achievements of the recent female sexual revolution is the distinction between virginity and hymen-preservation. From the faith point of view, virginity means the absence of all sexual relations before marriage. But from the late 1960s onwards, young women began to change their sexual behaviour. In 1975, I was leading a survey in Casablanca and a secondary-school student said to me: 'Making love without going too far, without penetration, is a reconciliation between my desire and the taboo.' That's a kind of compromise. She can please God by refusing to lose her hymen and, at the same time, she can give herself pleasure. The most recent survey by the Ministry of Health showed that 56% of young people between fifteen and twenty-four practise sex without penetration and 25% practise with penetration.

For these young people, non-penetrative sex remains a sin, but it's a minor one. This is their own distinction. On the other hand, fornication is a serious sin. The hymen is, in a manner of speaking, the female body's capital city: it must be preserved like an inviolable fortress. But it's also capital in that it allows us to measure a girl's worth. In poorer districts, the girls often possess no other capital. To spin out the metaphor, we could say that the body is like a nation state that will be defeated if its capital falls. If a girl loses that, she has lost everything. Moroccan men tend to believe that a woman's body is forever marked by her first partner. What's more, there are texts by the fuqaha, the 'scholars of the law', that say: 'Marry a virgin for fear the other woman cannot shake her lover.' Unfortunately, women submit to this imperative; they have their hymens restored or accept anal penetration instead. Ultimately, the victim and her tormenter are trapped by the same logic, and they perpetuate it.

Islam offers two solutions: premarital abstinence or early marriage, from the point of puberty. These days, both solutions have become unrealistic and unworkable. We cannot ask young people to abstain from sex between puberty and whenever they marry, which for boys is on average at thirty-one. So we devise a spatio-sexual kind of DIY. We hide in cars, on staircases, on roof terraces, on beaches and in the forest. And we are also going

'Ultimately, the victim and her tormenter are trapped by the same logic, and they perpetuate it.'

Heath Robinson in our approach to sex itself, since the hymen must be preserved. So this sex carries many risks: there are the social and health risks, the risk of pregnancy, of loss of the hymen, of arrest by the police and, of course, the risk of violence. The state is forced to attend to only one of these risks:

HIV, the management of which it delegates to charities, since those most affected are homosexuals and prostitutes, who already live on the wrong side of the law.

Society ignores all this. We tell people: 'Hide yourselves, keep your hymen and don't cause a scandal.' As soon as something is public, we condemn it. There is tolerance for all acts as long as they remain secret. I sum it all up in three words: 'Quiet, we're fucking.' Sex for young people is clandestine, and whatever is clandestine is wretched. We cannot live well when we're afraid, when we feel guilty. This is what we mean by 'sexual deprivation'.

The feminist movements neglect the sex question. They're afraid of losing credibility over it, of getting their hands dirty, as are the political parties. All the pressure sources come together to keep themselves and everyone else quiet. When we talk to progressives, so many of them insist that we must not go too fast or too far, for fear of sowing tension where public opinion is deeply attached to traditional ways – tradition in this case meaning the oppression of women. Unfortunately, in Morocco, the citizen has not yet supplanted the subject. A few years ago, the leader of the left-wing USFP party said that it was for the state to intervene against lechers and fornicators. I can't help feeling deeply troubled to hear this statesman of the left speaking the language of the conservatives.

There are a few unallied, minority voices that are beginning to speak out. I myself am marginalised, I struggle to publish my books in Morocco and I am often insulted and threatened. There are those who are working to eliminate clandestine abortion or

Aids or to promote the rights of single mothers. They are asking only for the right to sexual health, in a vague and somewhat confused way. But actually, we cannot fudge the issue of legalising sex outside marriage. First of all we must demand the right to sex! Once we have this right in place, we can work on sex education and awareness-raising programmes.

Few of us take responsibility for our actions: everyone wants to project a respectable image of themselves. We must reform these laws, which, moreover, are only very selectively applied. Even in the case of sex work, the police carry out raids among the poor prostitutes, the ones who walk the streets in their djellabas. If you have money and connections, you risk almost nothing. Unlike some observers, I don't believe that sexual deprivation was one of the triggers of 2011's Arab Spring. But such deprivation certainly gives rise to a feeling of frustration. Sexual modernity is inaccessible to the urban masses. And this feeds religious fundamentalism. As we cannot possess it, we want total control over the female body. It must be constantly under surveillance and constantly punished.

Dialmy concluded by reciting La Fontaine's fable of the frustrated fox who slanders the grapes when he cannot reach them, illustrating Dialmy's words to a T:

A fox of Gascon, though some say of Norman descent,
When starved till faint gazed up at a trellis to which
  grapes were tied —

Matured till they glowed with a purplish tint
As though there were gems inside.

Now grapes were what our adventurer on strained
haunches chanced to crave.
But because he could not reach the vine
He said, 'These grapes are sour; I'll leave them for
some knave.'
Better, I think, than an embittered whine.

RIM

'COOK, HAVE CHILDREN AND TAKE GOOD CARE OF YOUR HUSBAND'

I met Rim in November 2014, in Casablanca, at a literary cafe discussion about my novel. I was charmed by this bubbly woman. Six months later I wrote to her again and described my project. She agreed to contribute straight away.

Sex in Morocco is sick. Moroccan men have a problem with women, and this leads to lots of violence and imbalance. Only as they grow older, by reading books and watching films, do women realise that what they're experiencing with their husbands is not right. At eighteen, I didn't know anything. I was completely naive. I'd had zero sexual education. That was more than taboo: it didn't exist.

'Sex in Morocco is sick. Only as they grow older, by reading books and watching films, do women realise that what they're experiencing with their husbands is not right.'

My first husband was a violent, unhinged man. I had kept my virginity until marriage because that's how we were brought up, my two sisters and I. Virginity was compulsory. Nothing happened on the evening of our wedding. The next day I told my parents, who we were living with: 'He didn't touch me.' We went on for months like that. Each time, my parents came up with some excuse for him. My parents said I should look after him. And then, after a while, they began to tell me that sex wasn't at all important for a couple. They kept saying: 'God has chosen this for you.'

At that point, I started to go to the cinema and to read books. I gradually realised that this wasn't normal, that I didn't have to put up with it. We ended up having some sex, but it was always very brief and not at all satisfying. We had three children and our married life was truly hellish. My husband used to beat me and humiliate me. I couldn't see how to carry on with it. I left him and went to stay with my parents. At the time, the Family Code hadn't been reformed and I knew that care of my children would go to him. That was unbearable. My parents didn't support me at all – quite the opposite. They blamed me for leaving. My divorce brought shame on them. They knew that he'd been beating me, they saw the bruises on my face and body, but they accused me of lying. They let me stay for two days, then sent me back to my own place. It was torture with my children: I'd go to see them at school, I did everything to stay in touch with them. I only left to save myself from him.

I had no better luck with my second husband, who was a violent alcoholic. He used to rape me regularly. He would bring prostitutes into our home and tell me: 'You're lucky – I could go and marry three other women. I pick up a girl from time to time, I haven't humiliated you by taking another wife. You ought to thank me.'

During my second marriage, I had an affair. When we made love, I realised for the first time that what I was living with was truly awful. I had suggested to my first husband

that we consult a sexologist. But he was in complete denial.
He said over and over: 'It's because of you that I'm like this.'
When I was going to remarry, my parents said, 'Go and sleep
with him before you marry him. Otherwise you'll come back
full of complaints again.' So I did. But I didn't really have anything to compare it to. He seemed normal to me, although in
fact our sex was really terrible.

At thirty-eight, I was divorced again. I took some time out
to understand my life and I realised that, even though my
parents were loving, I had become a victim of their beliefs.
And that it wasn't just bad luck that I'd met such men. For
my own children, I wanted to offer them the opposite of what
I'd had. I talk to them about everything. I've brought up my
daughter free from this cult of virginity. I've taken her to the
gynaecologist, she has the pill. I've also talked to her myself
about how to protect against abuse and being touched.

I come from a social class that is well-to-do but not well
educated. My parents didn't plan for their daughters to go to
university. At eighteen, we had to get married. We had no
say in the matter. 'You must cook, have children and take
good care of your husband' – that's all I was brought up to
do. When things were going badly, they said, 'It's your destiny'
or 'There's something wrong with you.' At forty, I went back
to university, to study psychology, and for the last ten years I
haven't stopped studying.

Today, as a qualified therapist, I see a lot of women. I've
realised that Moroccan women cultivate a degree of patience
bordering on stupidity! They are capable of accepting the

unacceptable. Next to the things I hear, my own experience seems minor in comparison. Violence is practically a standard feature, whether by fathers or husbands. Young girls are often humiliated, belittled next to their brothers. This hardly prepares them for happy relationships with men. Many mothers who suffer in their marriages take their feelings out on their children. They make their sons into exemplars, into substitute husbands. Take my own example: my brother is four years younger than me but I was always made to call him 'sidi', which means 'monsieur'. I'm constantly wondering about how mothers are bringing up their boys. What values, what view of women, are they passing on to their children? It's very taboo to talk about the mother's role here, but I believe it's essential to call it out when mothers are passing their frustrations on to their children.

Among my girlfriends we talk about sex all the time. We are breaking the silence our parents imposed on us. It's a big awakening and it's wonderful! Besides, all my friends say the same thing: Moroccan men know nothing about foreplay. They're all about their own pleasure. And afterwards they stand up, take a shower and that's it. There is no romance, no communication, no delicacy. Many women feel like they've been raped when they have sex.

My daughter also had a nightmare experience. Her first husband forced her to stay indoors, to be the perfect housewife. She got divorced, with one baby. Now she's going to remarry but, as the law dictates, she will automatically lose the care of her child. Her husband immediately took the child's passport away. You could argue it's a way of saying that women can't change their lives. I am so angry. There are many, many divorces now that women have the right to initiate proceedings. They know that other situations are possible elsewhere; they aren't imprisoned as they used to be. But because cohabitation isn't permitted, people marry when they don't even know each other. And on the whole they don't like what they find. I have to say that I know very few contented couples.

Yet I'm still optimistic. We are in the midst of lancing more than one boil. Before, we didn't even talk about it. And women are seizing their rights; we're not waiting for them to be served up on a plate. After my divorces, I cohabited for five years and I never found it a problem. My parents were very unhappy, but I enjoyed rebelling. Now I travel, I read and I feel free. Women who don't work and who are financially dependent are forced to accept situations that can be appalling. I had a father with plenty of money. It's thanks to that that I've been able to survive.

SANAA EL AJI

'HAVE NO FEAR OF GOD . . . BUT ABOVE ALL FEAR THE GAZE OF OTHER PEOPLE'

Sanaa El Aji is a brilliant journalist and columnist. Among other publications, she has worked for the Arabic weekly *Nichane*, for which, famously, she contributed the diary entries of a curious and freethinking young divorcée called Batoul – with her committed feminism, as unlike Bridget Jones as UK readers can imagine, Batoul was nonetheless almost as well known. I met El Aji in Casablanca in June 2015.

I am often criticised for writing solely about sex and religion. In fact, I write about Moroccans' relationship with religion, about the gap between what we say and what we do, and so it's really about issues of personal freedom. In Morocco, we're over the old taboo around politics – we can talk about almost anything we want. The two new taboos are religion and sex. People get hysterical about them.

For my thesis ('Sexualité préconjugale au Maroc: représentations, verbalisation, pratiques et socialisation genrée' – 'Premarital Sex in Morocco: Representations, Verbalisation, Practices and Gendered Socialisation'*), which relates directly to these questions, I interviewed people across Morocco and I can assure you that not a single person I met could say: 'I've never done anything.' The boys mostly say they want a virgin wife. If they fall in love with a girl who isn't a virgin, some say* *they could forgive her, they could even move to a new town for her. For them, if a women is not a virgin, she must either be a prostitute or she's been deceived, she's a victim. They're incapable of imagining that she has quite simply been living her own life, that she's been enjoying herself. And the girls absolutely don't want virgin husbands. There's a whole chapter in my thesis about the different values attached to virginity, depending on whether it's in men or women.*

People have taken social prohibitions on board and adapted them in their own ways. The girls play the timid virgin. For example, the first time they have sex with a man, they don't move. Lots of them have heard awful stories about men attacking their partners, saying, 'Where did you learn to do that?' Girls have a range of options they can fall back on: anal sex, fellatio, etc. – anything as long as they keep their hymen intact. And again we see virginity defined not as a state of chastity but as a physical attribute – an unbroken hymen.

Yes, I do upset some people, but I must say that lots of people also want to thank me, to say 'We weren't brave enough to say that.' What shocks me is the total absence of any nuance whenever we start thinking about sex, whether hetero- or homosexual. For many men (and women too, sometimes), there's nothing between the virtuous woman and the prostitute. They have a strongly Manichaean view of women. As for virginity, when I say that that's not what determines a woman's value, they accuse me of wanting to turn all women into prostitutes. That said, I must also admit I've never been blocked from publishing anything; I've been able to communicate all my craziest ideas. I don't censor myself at all and no one else has censored me either.

I come from a modest background. I grew up in a working-class area and my education was fairly traditional. My parents are pious people – not overly conservative, but I was still brought up with the traditional principles of virginity, marriage, children . . . Then, at twenty-six, I went to live by myself, which was very, very unusual at the time. I did it spontaneously, without weighing up what it meant in the context of my education. It's clear to me now that that choice had a positive impact on my personal development and maturity.

I don't know precisely what lies behind my freedom. Of course reading has opened my mind to the world. I was lucky to go to public secondary schools, where there were lots of extra activities, but I don't recall any particular turning point. I always had a rebellious personality. I used to say no. I dared to stand firm against things that didn't work for me. There are no taboos in my writing. Sometimes I'm the one who's on the warpath. This way I can – occasionally – protect myself by actively provoking others. I think I must have accidentally come up with this self-defence system: when you're leading the attack, people think twice before attacking you back. I live as I like; it's my own life. I don't hide behind appearances or smoke-screen statements. Those close to me understand. Not everyone is a frustrated lunatic. The most important thing for me is to be honest with myself; to live in line with how I see things.

I have nine brothers and sisters, and I'm the first girl in the family to receive the baccalaureate. Our parents remember

Morocco's Years of Lead, the oppression experienced from the 1960s until the 1990s, and sometimes they worry about our freedom and what we're up to. But one day my father told me: 'I'm proud of you' – and I'll never forget that.

My research has shown me that all Moroccans have a sex life. Only the circumstances differ. What's interesting is seeing how young people are handling the difference between the official line and reality, how they get around the constraints. Some of the boys will explain that they masturbate before going to see a prostitute. This helps them avoid premature ejaculation. Sometimes boys will indulge in group masturbation competitions. And then there's the cinema – another place for sex. In Tangier, I heard this wild story about a van that would drive around while couples had sex in the back. There's a creativity, a fabulous sense of humour, that goes into inventing new spaces for sex. I'm also very interested in 'how you say it', I mean the language of sex, which is mostly very crude and violent. We're shocked when women swear – yet men in the street regularly use absolutely eye-watering insults on us.

I remember an Egyptian film in which the Moroccan actress Sanaa Akroud stepped out of an unmade bed where a bloodstain was visible on the sheets. It caused a scandal here. People said that she brought shame on Moroccans. If she'd been a man, there'd have been no problem! But Moroccans are obsessed by the behaviour of 'their women': we're like ambassadors for the national virtue and our national identity.

When I was a child, nobody told us about periods or our bodies. And so many girls thought they'd lost their virginity when they saw that first menstrual blood. *The boys' sex edu-cation amounts to no more than a virility contest. They boast about having done this or that, and I think it completely screws up their perspective on things. I read a study which showed that the first sexual experience happens later in countries with a sex education programme, in com-parison with countries without any sex education. The secrecy, the taboo around it, ultimately creates the opposite effect to what's intended: we're all desperate to find out what it is we're not meant to know.*

In Casablanca and in the big cities generally, more and more independent women are taking ownership of their sex lives. They will talk straightforwardly about sex, without false modesty. But most of them stick at foreplay, no pene-tration. Many of them have their hymens restored so they can still take part in this

'How many women have told me: "I did it because he promised to marry me"? Men always choose, above all, not to marry a woman who's agreed to have a sexual relationship with them.'

reinforcement of patriarchal dominance. They are perpetu-ating a lie, a hypocrisy, and they find it very hard to take responsibility for sexual intercourse itself. How many women have told me: 'I did it because he promised to marry me'? Men always choose, above all, not to marry a woman who's agreed to have a sexual relationship with them.

Men are not our enemies in this battle. They too are suf-fering with this malaise, these ambiguities. They too would like relationships with women to be simpler. Let's be honest

*and acknowledge that women also see a commercial value
to their bodies. For many of them, their husband primarily
offers social advancement. The man brings a dowry as com-
pensation for the marriage. There is also the concept of r'chim
or mahr, a kind of advance dowry gift paid before the engage-
ment, as if to 'reserve' the wife-to-be. This may seem shocking.
Indeed, in one of my radio essays I compared this practice to
the custom of branding a cow in order to reserve it, to say:
'That one's mine.' Yet I've known female doctors, senior female
managers, who measure their value in terms of the presents
they receive. In a way, their marriage is a form of institutionalised prostitution: the man has to pay, often a substantial
sum, to be able to 'own' a certain woman. The more he pays,
the more highly she is valued. Many women yearn for modernity but at the same time they want their husband to earn the
money and look after them. Very few really take 'modernity'
on board. There are a lot of contradictions but mainly a serious lack of intellectual honesty. On both sides, the arguments
are horribly lacking in coherence. We have reduced 'modernity' to not much at all.*

*One day, I took part in a TV programme all about sex-
ual harassment. I addressed all the men who harass women,
saying, broadly: If you can't keep a lid on your instincts, that
makes you the animals. When I got home, it was already out
of control. My Facebook wall was flooded with aggressive
comments and abuse. They called me a whore, they insulted
me. People were saying: 'How can you stand for sexual freedom and be against harassment?' To think they refused to see*

that the two things have absolutely nothing to do with each other. Another time, a journalist interviewing me about personal freedom asked me: 'What is your position on porn films and the sexual abuse of children?' It's as if defending people's freedoms as individuals means endorsing pornography and paedophilia.

People really find it difficult to understand individuals' rights and freedoms. When you defend homosexuality, you're accused of wanting to turn all Moroccans gay or of encouraging moral decadence. Society only cares that no one knows what 'bad' things we're doing. Its slogan is simple: 'Have no fear of God, far less for your own values, but above all fear the gaze of other people.' Don't go rocking the boat – that's all.

MOUNA

'THERE'S NO LIFE FOR GAY WOMEN IN MOROCCO'

I've known Mouna for a few years; she has never hidden her homosexuality. Now and then we've discussed how she feels about Morocco. Several times she's expressed her sense of repugnance at the conservative attitudes here, and at the interference of society and family in individuals' private lives. Over the winter of 2015, I contacted her and asked if she would agree to speak on the record for me. After some consideration she agreed, on condition that I preserve her anonymity. I have, therefore, changed her name.

My father was a teacher and my mother didn't have a job. They are people of the left and open to modern ideas. They are also middle-class, and my whole education was through the public education system. My first memory connected to sex is of the day my mother came to fetch me from school, when I was twelve or thirteen. She said: 'When we get our period, we have a new body and we have to start taking more care. Men will look at you differently. You're not a little girl any more.' A year later, my father asked me if I knew what a condom was. 'Perhaps one day you will fall in love and you will want to try something new – there are risks.' Both of them were trying to find the best way of facing up to their children's maturing sexuality. My father spoke more freely than my mother; he gave words to things.

At school, my friends had to be home by sunset. They had very strict upbringings and most of their mothers wore hijab. In general, the girls led very protected lives. My father was more liberal. The first time I went to a nightclub, it was he who took me there and he came to collect me at three in the morning.

Ultimately, society was harsher than my parents. I felt secure at home. At secondary school, the headmaster wouldn't let me attend one day when my hair wasn't styled 'appropriately', according to him. I knew that the street was not a place for women. My game plan was to leave Morocco.

The first time I felt desire, I was seventeen: I read a book that had an erotic scene and I began to masturbate without even realising it. Following that, I went out with a boy. I had decided to lose my virginity. I asked him if he would like us to make love and he said no. I had to reassure him, promise I didn't want anything from him. In the end, we did it, the way I wanted to.

When I went abroad, my biggest surprise was at how much more straightforward, how much less concerned about money and appearances, the young people were there than in Morocco.

After I turned twenty-five, my mother started to become really difficult. Marriage became her main objective, especially now that people had started coming to ask for my hand. Of course, she said, 'You have to ask Mouna.' Like many mothers, her life was partly lived vicariously, through me. The main thing was that I enjoyed a liberty she'd never had, and *she had mixed feelings about this: she was both pleased for me and infuriated.*

The first time I fell in love, it was with a woman. I wasn't at all troubled. It felt natural for me. She was a foreigner, a very free woman, and I admired her enormously. I was very much in love, so I was happy. I only started to question my feelings after we broke up. I had told no one in the family apart from my brother. He was surprised but he didn't try to judge me at the time. Still, as years went by, he wouldn't stop asking me: 'So, when are you going to introduce us to someone?' I knew that by 'someone' he meant a man and that he thought my homosexuality had just been a phase, a childish whim.

I don't define myself as 'gay'. Actually, I don't have an identity: I've no gender or sexual orientation. I have never confined myself to these categories. I've never needed to fit myself into a box.

I didn't feel like a homosexual until the day I told my parents I was one. I thought there was no point hiding it and letting my mother go on dreaming about my wedding and all her grandchildren. Every day my mother was asking me: 'But doesn't anyone fancy you? This isn't normal. Why don't you approach boys?' It was becoming really oppressive. I had just turned thirty and there was no need for this lie any more. I didn't really anticipate the fallout from my bombshell. I thought she already knew about me but didn't want to admit it. For years my mother could see I'd had only girlfriends.

She took the news very badly. She started to pray – and she never used to pray. She said that God was punishing her. She blamed my father a lot, for having given us too free an education. She wanted to stop my sister from going abroad. For her, that had become the site of moral corruption and decadence. Then, after a month, she began to change completely. She turned very gentle. Now she thinks of me like a sick person, as if I'm disabled. She thinks I have a problem that can be fixed by her love and also by sessions with a psychiatrist. She is convinced a doctor will be able to cure me of this 'disease'.

'Everyone is hiding. Everyone is a hypocrite. We're living in a kind of doublethink, at every social level.'

I'm not an activist. I'm trying to change what's within my reach. But I'm still convinced there's no life for gay women in Morocco. The lesbians I know here are suffering, they're unhappy, even if they say they've accepted this life of secrecy. Here, the very notions of private life and personal space don't exist. People have to know who you're going out with, who you're marrying, everything you're doing . . . These days, people know what homosexuality is, they're aware of what's going on around them. But I feel that, paradoxically, this only makes them more aggressive. Homosexuality is for 'the others' – also known as westerners – not for us. It's fine for them but not for us. Even our sexuality is an aspect of our identity, and so always determined by our religion. We are set apart. People tell us: 'Don't do that in our country. Go and live somewhere else.' My father said that if I really thought this would be my *way of life, I would have to leave Morocco. He is very worried seeing me live here while openly asserting my homosexuality.*

I know I'm living in danger. But I also know that, if I keep quiet, no one's going to barge in on me. Ultimately, I feel the same as straight people, from that point of view. Everyone is hiding. Everyone is a hypocrite. We're living in a kind of doublethink, at every social level. As soon as I'm out of Morocco, I feel lighter.

I was chatting to one of my old school friends recently. She's a very pious woman, wears a headscarf and had never deviated from the path laid out for her. She married young. A few months after the wedding, she told me that she'd never had an orgasm. 'I don't like his body. His touch repels me.' When I expressed concern about this, she replied: 'It's not important.' In the end, their marriage lasted a year. She left him, and now she's seeing a man who fulfils her sexually. The woman has changed completely: now she is pro-abortion and supports women's right to control their own bodies; she has become much more feminist. She had been working the same hours as her husband and she'd had to handle all the household tasks. Before her marriage, she thought that was OK. But she couldn't bear the actual experience of it and the patent injustice of the situation.

I knew one girl who came out and for whom the consequences were much more terrible than for me. She's now been diagnosed as bipolar. She's lost her mind. At first, she'd tried to protect herself by marrying a friend who knew about her homosexuality. Except, once they were married, he started to pull the whole macho thing. He forbade her from going out. She came from a very modest background and her parents had borrowed money so that they could give her a fine wedding. She became dependent on her husband. When she confessed everything to her parents, they had her admitted to a psychiatric hospital. I tried to protect her. I offered to put her up, to help her. But I couldn't do anything. She was sedated all the time. Now she's lost her job, her friends and all contact with the outside world.

The internet has completely transformed social life for gay people. These days, it's much easier to meet people, though you still have to be careful. A few years ago I came across a site called LesbiennesdeRabat.com – 'RabatLesbians.com'. I couldn't believe it! It must have had a hundred or so women subscribing. Of course they were using photos of film stars and false names. The site's administrator was very paranoid. You really had to prove your credentials if you wanted to sign up. I decided to send my own photo in. That made her so suspicious that she refused to let me subscribe!

Another thing: the homosexual scene is without a doubt where you find the greatest social mix. There are bankers and bored housewives but also girls from very poor backgrounds.

In our society, as I'm not married, it looks strange that I don't stay at my parents' house every night. We grow up with this culture that 'everything is allowed in private', but there's only really one path that dominates. The time always comes

when you have to follow the herd. As you grow older, you realise that a life on the margins is too difficult. The price is too
high. I see my mother suffering and it eats at me. In fact, the
worst thing is that I can put myself in her shoes but she's unable to see things my way. Lots of gay people end up marrying
to save face. It doesn't seem absurd to me, I don't judge them.

At work, every day people ask me when I'm going to get
married. All day long I am given advice by women who are
shocked that I don't have children. As for the men, they only
half accept women's liberty. So many of them have said to me:
'We're already allowing our wives to have jobs and go about
without headscarves; what if they start having affairs?' At my
office, all the women wear hijab, some out of religious conviction and others for practical reasons. They say: 'We take the
bus, we go home late at night. If we don't wear our veils we're
sure to be attacked.' Weirdly, the veil is there to protect them
from the 'savages' in the street. From my colleagues' point of
view, men think about nothing but fucking and that's as it
should be. That adds up to a basically contradictory view, for
men represent both the danger and the source of protection. I
even know some women who say they'd be happy if their husband took a second wife, as that would relieve them of their
conjugal duties.

FEDWA MISK

'JUST BEING MYSELF IS ACTIVISM'

A doctor by training, Fedwa Misk soon discovered a passion for journalism. A freelance reporter for both Moroccan and foreign newspapers, blogger and chair of literary panel discussions, in 2011 she created the collaborative feminist webzine *Qandisha*. I met her at her Casablanca home in the summer of 2015.

Things are changing, slowly but surely. I feel as though we're managing to live together a little better. When, for example, I find myself confronting very conservative people, I think: 'Perhaps I won't make them change their minds. But I can make them accept me.' I've had to deal with these kind of people in my professional life and after a few years I realised that my relationships with them had been transformed. These people know me, they know I'm completely different from them, that I don't share their religious morality but I do have my own ethics. They understand that I'm not the devil and the fact that I don't match their criteria for a 'nice girl' isn't enough to write me off as evil. This is progress on a day-to-day level.

In the wake of the 20 February Movement, I created Qandisha, *a collaborative site that invites women and men to express opinions on the widest possible range of subjects. When the magazine launched, I really felt I was discovering people*

*like myself. We recognised each other and realised we weren't
alone. I remember getting a message from a young woman
saying: 'Thank you! You make me feel less mad.' She was from
Agadir, a small town in southern Morocco, where girls either
follow the traditions or they're considered whores. This young
woman had upset her neighbours by asking an office colleague
to come to her house in the evenings to work. In a letter to us,
she told of her confrontation with the police and the formal
accusations then made against her. If Qandisha has helped to
save just one woman, that's a great thing.*

*It's true that Moroccan society is badly divided. But we
have to stop trying to fit ourselves into other people's systems.
It isn't enough to drink wine and consider yourself the model
of modernity. On the contrary: I can assure you that some
women in hijab are actually very secular and very free with
their bodies. At the moment, Islamists are in power, yet there
hasn't been the catastrophe we were led to expect. We're keeping up the pressure, and we've even managed to make the
justice minister talk about reforming the laws on sex! Even
the last prime minister, Abdelilah Benkirane, spoke up on the
question of homosexuality, while many on the left still don't
even dare talk about it. I was able to interview Benkirane
personally, just before the elections. I said to him: 'I'm an
atheist, I drink alcohol and I have sex without being married.
What are you going to do about me?' He was dumbstruck for
a moment, then he replied: 'You can do what you like at home,
I don't care. But if I find you naked in the street, of course I'll
come and cover you up.'*

I grew up in El Jadida, a small town on the Atlantic coast. I can say that my mother was liberated in comparison with the women of her generation. She had a big character. She brought us up practically by herself, as my father was hardly there. She was my model. She was a firm leader, head of a secondary school with dozens of men in her employment. She was fiercely opposed to the headscarf. She used to receive male friends at our house. She'd go shopping with a work colleague in Casablanca – and she was always respected by her peers. Nobody was shocked. She had us late – her first daughter at twenty-nine – and she always said that motherhood was not the be-all and end-all for her. This was very rare, especially in her time and milieu. I have black-and-white photos of her in a miniskirt. We mustn't be naive, and she herself used to tell me that she did get harassed. But she would step in to calm the men down, whether in the street or at work. Several of them became her good friends. My mother was nonetheless very strict. She brought up her three children by herself and her word was the law.

I left El Jadida for Casablanca and to begin studying medicine. I was sharing an apartment at the time. The other tenants were often afraid of the boys who bothered us and the neighbours who harassed us. The agent of the building wouldn't talk to us, only to the landlord. More often than not I was the one who found a solution.

Casablanca is a monster city; it changes you. At first the city frightened me, more than it gave me any sense of freedom. In El Jadida, everything is small and reassuring, everyone knows everyone. Casablanca is a sprawling metropolis. But then I began to meet people, to go beyond the limited circuit of the medical students. I started to shift the invisible barriers that I hadn't dared cross before. I had a few eureka moments, particularly in my reading.

Sex is everywhere we go, but it takes place within a very patriarchal setting. The men boast about their conquests, while women overplay the discretion card and lie much of the time. At the veterinary faculty, I know there's a mixed dorm where it used to be wild, but in medicine, communication between the girls and the boys was still generally quite discreet. Anyway, it's in a girl's interests to protect her reputation. If a girl doesn't marry the man she is sleeping with, things could go very wrong for her. Luckily, Casablanca is vast. In the small towns, it's much tougher.

My partner is a foreigner, which can be problematic. Sometimes the doorman says to me: 'Your cousin rang but you weren't in.' Although he knows it wasn't my cousin – particularly as he's blond with straight hair! The other day it was a streetseller who said: 'I know all about you, you know. And I've seen your husband, the foreigner.' I was so angry that I replied: 'Really? Which one?' He shut up but went on grinning.

I know there are risks for me. Not long ago, I was arrested in my car one evening with a writer friend whose wife is my best friend. The police just wanted to tap us for some cash. We'd done absolutely nothing wrong. So the cop said to my friend: 'You know you're risking your home and family for that . . . ?' pointing to me with a look of disgust. I got out of the car and asked him: 'What do you mean by "that"?' I think you have to show that you know your rights, that you refuse to be humiliated. I was ready to go to the police station if necessary.

I know they can call on article 490 – our sword of Damocles – whenever they want. But actually, you have to go quite far to get yourself arrested for a moral offence. I think they only act on it when you're really too visible, too difficult for those around you. Usually everything can be resolved through negotiation. People are already living with poverty and un-employment; you can't impose too much police pressure on their private lives as well.

I do try not to self-censor, not to give in to the pressures. Just being myself is activism, in a way. I feel as though it's my duty to set an example. I'd love to introduce you to Ito, my cleaning lady, one day. She's a wonderful woman. She lives in Sidi Moumen and she's traditional. She knows Alex, my part-ner, and she knows me well too. I think she's no longer shocked by my lifestyle these days. Sometimes we sit down, the two of us, and chat for hours. I ask her why she stays with her hus-band, who just hangs around and doesn't work and frustrates her. I tell her that she's beautiful and could find someone else. That makes her laugh but I know what she's really thinking. She's thirty-nine and she thinks her life is over.

One day Alex said to me, 'I'd really like to go for a walk with you somewhere you're allowed to show signs of affec-tion.' I was gobsmacked. I genuinely hadn't realised I was so tense with him in public. Morocco has a massive emotional *drought, a real problem with affection. People are frustrated. We think the internet and the social networks will help open people's minds. But being able to see everything that's going*

'Look at the prostitutes: they never stop going on about religion.'

on doesn't guarantee open-mindedness. Instead it leads to more frustration. When we speak out for sexual freedom, people accuse us of wanting to turn Morocco into one big brothel. That infuriates me, but at the same time I understand, because that's the culture I come from. My family was conservative and religious; I too grew up with those expectations of virginity and marriage.

The first time I had intercourse, it was entirely my decision; it was a choice. Most girls don't make that decision. They go out with a guy, and then it happens in the heat of the moment and they feel very guilty about it. Look at the prostitutes: they never stop going on about religion. Often a prostitute will conclude that she's the one at fault and she'll hope that, one day, she'll be able to expiate her sins and be saved. If I then tell her that I had sex in full knowledge of the facts and that I don't feel guilty, she may not understand. She'll be horrified! What's shocking is that I don't feel ashamed, that I'm not obsessed with the notion of getting back on the 'right path'. However much we explain that we only ever have sex in line with our own ethics, they don't care: morality is religious or it isn't morality. You have to live with that. I don't care how other people live, but I will not let anyone force me into anything.

SAMIRA

'I DIDN'T GIVE MYSELF MUCH FREEDOM. I WISH I'D HAD THE COURAGE TO MAKE DISCOVERIES'

Samira wrote me a message on Facebook. One of her girl-friends had told her about my project and she wanted to take part. We met in a cafe in Rabat, in November 2015.

I was always quite shy – or prudish, perhaps. It's because of both my education and my personality. As a teenager I found it very hard to imagine going out with someone of my own age. I wouldn't make the first move, I was a bit closed off. I have three brothers who never put pressure on me and never tried to control me. On the contrary: they were open-minded and easy-going; I could even go out to nightclubs with them.

My parents are cultured people, interested in everything. They gave us a traditional education but also one that was relatively critical towards the status quo. From their point of view, modesty is a natural quality, it's biological. They think we have to accept a number of cultural norms so that we'll behave appropriately in society – particularly in relation to the opposite sex. Now I realise that I'm recreating with my own children how my mother was with me. I'm always tell-ing my daughter to sit properly and keep her legs together. Perhaps I'm giving her inhibitions without meaning to.

I studied at the law school in Rabat. It wasn't easy. I came from the French lycée and I had real problems adapting. The students from more working-class and more traditional back-grounds didn't at all have the same outlook as my friends and me. They were quite narrow-minded and when we talked about taboo topics – sex, for example – they could be quite shocked. I remember we used to hide behind a tree when we wanted to smoke. You had to hide the whole time – especially when it came to boy–girl relationships. Couples formed, they'd meet up, make love, but from the outside you wouldn't see a thing. People don't show their relationships, they can't flourish in this society.

Young people today are more open than we are, they're more rebellious. I think things are getting better and better, compared with what people claim, at least. We have a new habit of speaking out. In my childhood, we only had hshouma, even within the family. We didn't talk about love or sex. Among brothers and sisters, OK, a little. But with my father that wasn't possible. We didn't dare. These days, I think people are talking more about these things. The issue of virginity is not as taboo as it used to be. People understand that everyone has to live their own life. And it has to be said that women are taking more responsibility for their lives. Among my friends, I know several who aren't afraid to talk about sex or even to make their relationships public.

As for me, I stayed a virgin until I was married. I can't say for sure if that was my choice or because of my educa-tion. Anyway, I wanted there to be a real, spiritual connection with my first partner. Unlike what you might think, it wasn't easy staying a virgin. Even though it's the official norm in *our society, the reality is quite different. I didn't have many friends who made the same choices as me. They tried to pressure me. I got a bit of teasing. They told me 'You're uptight' or 'Go on, strike while you're hot.' But I was scared and I never took the plunge. I wouldn't say I suffered but when I think back on it now, I realise that I didn't give myself much freedom. I wish I'd had the courage to make discoveries, to be led simply by pleasure. What can you do . . .*

My husband turned out to have had some experience and I agreed he could tell me about it. Honestly, it wasn't a problem for me – I wasn't jealous about his past. Quite sincerely, I know he wouldn't have been able to marry a woman who wasn't a virgin. The girls he used to see and who he slept with mostly weren't from the same social set as him. They tended to be more working-class girls, who didn't have much education. Anyway, he couldn't have married any of them. I think that for him there was a very clear distinction between the woman he would marry and the ones with whom he'd have his sexual education.

'There are things I would never dare ask him. And there are also things he wouldn't like to see me do. For him, I am first and foremost his children's mother and I think that some sexual practices would appear degrading to him.'

To be completely honest, I'm still quite shy on that front, even though I love my husband and we've been a strong couple for nearly twelve years now. There are things I would never dare ask him. And there are also things he wouldn't like to see me do. For him, I am first and foremost his children's mother and I think that some sexual practices would appear degrading to him. Things I don't dare say here but which aren't for 'nice girls' to do. I say that in quote marks because I don't judge anybody and I do think everyone has the right to do what they wish with their body. Really, it's society that makes this kind of distinction.

CONCLUSION

In 2016, after the New Year's Eve sex attacks in Cologne, Algerian journalist Kamel Daoud published an opinion piece that drew heavy criticism. He saw the Arab Muslim world as riddled – scarred, even – by sexual deprivation. The young people were stifled by the burden of their frustrations, which led to explosions of aggression upon contact with women, whether in Tahrir Square, or in Cologne, or, as we have seen, in the streets of Moroccan cities. French intellectuals claimed in response that Daoud was guilty of spreading 'orientalist clichés' and that he was stereotyping the Arab masses. Perhaps. I do understand that these intellectuals prefer to preach caution from the safe distance of their faculty offices in France. But it nonetheless seems to me impossible to deny the reality of sexual deprivation as a social fact, a vast problem and one whose effects clearly impact on the political realm.

When I was working at *Jeune Afrique*, I had opportunities to report from Algeria and from Tunisia under the presidency of Zine Ben Ali. I regularly covered issues relating to young people and, every time, I sensed the malaise among this section of the population who were unable to lead their sex lives safely and with dignity. How many young Algerian and Tunisian men have confessed to me that, on top of dealing with unemployment, humiliation and the absence of any leisure opportunities, they were suffering horribly from being unable to see their girlfriends, unable to spend any time with them, unable to claim any right to privacy? I'd love to invite these furious intellectuals to a working-class bar in Casablanca or Tangier for an evening. I took myself out to one again a few months ago and I must say the scene was tragic. A gloomy, smoky room in which only men and a few prostitutes sit round the tables. The young people there hardly talk. They work their way through bottle after bottle of Morocco's Spéciale beer, and watch whichever of the girls is dancing. When I stepped into this bar, the waiter was worried about me. He wondered what I thought I was doing there. He told me, blushing, in a tone both gentle and patronising, that this was not a place for 'nice girls'. But I sat down anyway. I kept my face cool, unmoved. For a while I observed the barmaid working there; she was a youngish, rather plump woman. I wanted to talk to her but the manager made it plain that she was there to work, not to make conversation. That evening, I sadly observed the total lack of interaction between the sexes. In this bar, it was clear that male–female relationships would be possible only on condition of financial exchange.

As the political commentator and former chief editor of *TelQuel* Abdellah Tourabi pointed out to me, 'We could analyse the question of sex in Morocco through a quasi-Marxist lens and say that sexual deprivation is moving in parallel with social deprivation. These days, a young person with a house, a car and income can lead their sex life however they like, even if their preference is, in fact, illegal. But a young person from the poor parts of town will hardly have a sex life, and what they do have will be beset by risk and doubtless very unfulfilling.' Then he made a comparison with football matches, which, in Morocco, can often spark bursts of violence. 'At the end of a match, young people take their anger out on two things: cars and women. Two things they're unable to possess and upon which they vent their frustration.' According to Tourabi, even when they have access to greater freedom, Moroccans behave 'like emotional parvenus': they have no idea what to do with their feelings or their freedom. Hence the stratospheric divorce rate and the extreme tensions between men and women.

Although I don't think that financial security can completely quell our sense of arbitrariness, and even a Moroccan with financial resources will suffer from this lack of sexual freedom, I am sure Tourabi is right. Sexual deprivation sits within the wider context of young people's social deprivation: a picture that includes unemployment, the absence of any cultural life, decreased access to Europe and the rise of fundamentalist Islamism. We might turn here to sociologist Pierre Bourdieu's definition of social deprivation, which is not merely an 'ordinary suffering', caused by insufficient resources and material poverty. In his study *The Weight of the World*, Bourdieu speaks rather of 'positional suffering', in which individuals' legitimate aspirations to happiness and personal fulfilment constantly come up against obstructions and laws that are beyond their control.

Be that as it may, if these testimonies confirm one thing, it's the fact that this sexual deprivation isn't caused solely by the dominance either of particular moral values or of religion in Morocco. It appears clearly to have political, economic and social origins and effects. The widespread sexual deprivation affects women, young people and the poor in particular. It lies at the heart of a system that resists reform and that continues to generate ever worse abuses. The tension between the desire for modernity and the attachment – whether genuine or superficial – to traditional values is wearing down Moroccan society. And, at the root of this tension, the stakes are no less than the emergence of the individual. If laws relating to sexual freedoms are not applied or are poorly applied by the authorities, the most fanatical citizens do not hesitate to take justice into their own hands. As anthropologist Mohamed-Sghir Janjar explained in one television appearance, 'Social groups are trying to re-establish a moral order they judge to be under threat. They are fighting against what they believe to be attempts to undermine civilisation!' I have repeated several times that there's a flagrant disparity between the number of people considered to be 'guilty' and the actual application of the laws in criminal charges. We mustn't, then, be inclined to forget that, right now, adulterous women and homosexuals are serving very real sentences inside Moroccan prisons. It's the weakest, the poorest and the most marginalised that fate ultimately strikes. These humiliated people, these offenders, are condemned for their sexual orientation, for a single sex act or for one kiss too many, according not to the danger they present to society but rather to a morality that's both penny-pinching and vague.

All these testimonies also confirm the central role that women play in these issues. Despite our legislative advances, despite the progress made by Moroccan society, women's bodies are still controlled by the group. Before she can be an individual, a woman must be a mother, a sister, a wife, a daughter. She is the guarantee of family honour and, worse still, of the nation's identity. Her virtue is a public matter. Therefore, we still need to invent the woman who belongs to no one; who will answer for her actions only as citizen A or B, and not according to her sex; the woman who can live independently of the *qa'ida*, which is to say, independently of the norms, the customs

We still need to invent the woman who belongs to no one.

of patriarchy. 'Many of the things people enjoyed doing most in life, like walking around, discovering the world, singing, dancing and expressing an opinion, often turned up in the "strictly forbidden to women" category. Women's happiness violates the *qa'ida*,' as Fatima Mernissi wrote.

Of the women I met, there were many who were moving beyond the rules and customs, and even beyond the reach of others' opinions. These women are, I hope, my country's future. They are not waiting to be given the space to live their lives. They are taking what's there to be taken; they're asserting their thirst for freedom even while the price they'll pay for it remains high. I would hate, above all, to confine them to the category of victims. In the absence of role models, they are inventing themselves anew. And I've been struck by the extraordinary creativity of girls and boys alike as they invent spaces for love and sex. As for men, they are not all enemies of this freedom. True, they are disconcerted by the speed with which Moroccan women have adapted to change and modernisation. But they nonetheless aspire too to love and freedom. It remains for the legislators to do all they can so that each and every person, no matter their personal concept of virtue or purity, is able to lead their own sexual life safely and with dignity.

The Kamel Daoud business is sadly not an isolated incident. Personally I am no longer surprised when, in trying to advocate progress, I am accused of sowing the seeds of fundamentalism, of helping to consolidate Islamists' resolve a little more every time I open my mouth. I am accused of opportunistic Islamophobia and of not respecting Morocco's traditional values. And finally, the clinching argument: they say I have sold out to the West. My detractors come in many guises: they are from Islamist movements or from western far-right tendencies; some are superficially progressive but more attached to their privileges than to their supposed values, and some are embittered conservatives who advocate a kind of identity purism. In his lyrical final book, *J'avais tant de choses à dire encore . . . – I Still Had So Many Things to Say . . .* – Malek Chebel wrote: 'To work on the sex taboo, the taboo of women's emancipation, that of desire and especially that of free speech, could only bring me rebuffs. Even those

I believed I was defending – women, the young, unmarried people – only partially understood. All have judged me and all were enraged that I had so completely freed myself of the bonds still choking them practically to death. As with every liberation, the erotic and above all the right to speak about it can only be won by bitter struggle. And this relies upon a rare freedom: the right to think for oneself. We must confront this most monumental taboo of all.'

BIBLIOGRAPHY

Chimamanda Ngozi Adichie, *We Should All Be Feminists* (Vintage Books, 2014)

Salwa Al Neimi, *The Proof of the Honey* (Europa Editions, 2009)

Tahar Ben Jelloun, *La Plus Haute des solitudes* (Seuil, 1997)

Sophie Bessis, *Les Arabes, les femmes, la liberté* (Albin Michel, 2007)

Abdelwahab Bouhdiba, *Sexuality in Islam* (Routledge & Kegan Paul, 1985)

Malek Chebel, *J'avais tant de choses à dire encore* (Éditions Desclée de Brouwer, 2017)

Malek Chebel, *L'Érotisme arabe* (Robert Laffont, 2014)

Malek Chebel, *L'Inconscient de l'islam: Réflexions sur l'interdit, la faute et la transgression* (CNRS, 2015)

Malek Chebel, *Le Kama-Sutra arabe: 2000 ans de littérature érotique en Orient* (Pauvert, 2006)

Abdessamad Dialmy, *Sexualité et discours au Maroc* (Afrique Orient, 1988)

Shereen El Feki, *Sex and the Citadel: Intimate Life in a Changing Arab World* (Chatto & Windus, 2013)

Mona Eltahawy, *Headscarves and Hymens: Why the Middle East Needs a Sexual Revolution* (Weidenfeld & Nicolson, 2015)

Michel Foucault, *The History of Sexuality, Volume I: An Introduction* (Random House, 1978)

Joumana Haddad, *I Killed Scheherazade: Confessions of an Angry Arab Woman* (Saqi Books, 2010)

Joumana Haddad, *Superman is an Arab: On God, Marriage, Macho Men and Other Disastrous Inventions* (The Westbourne Press, 2012)

Asma Lamrabet, *Women in the Qur'an: An Emancipatory Reading* (Square View, 2016)

O. Z. Livaneli, *Bliss* (St. Martin's Press, 2007)

Fatima Mernissi, *Dreams of Trespass: Tales of a Harem Girlhood* (Addison-Wesley, 1994)

Fatima Mernissi, *L'Amour dans les pays musulmans* (Albin Michel, 2009)

Fatima Mernissi, *The Veil and the Male Elite: A Feminist Interpretation of Women's Rights in Islam* (Perseus Books, 1991)

Nedjma, *The Almond: The Sexual Awakening of a Muslim Woman* (Grove Atlantic, 2005)

Abdelhak Serhane, *L'Amour circoncis* (Paris-Méditerranée, 2000)

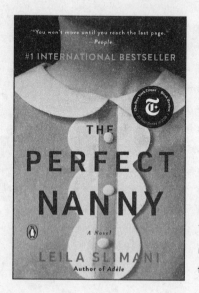